A Geography of
19th-Century Britain

A Geography of 19th-Century Britain

P. J. Perry

Reader in Geography, University of Canterbury,
Christchurch, New Zealand

B. T. Batsford Ltd,
London & Sydney

First published 1975

Copyright © P. J. Perry, 1975

Printed and bound in Great Britain by
Redwood Burn Ltd, Trowbridge and Esher
for the publishers,
B. T. Batsford Ltd, 4 Fitzhardinge Street, London W1 and
23 Cross Street, Brookvale, N.S.W. 2100, Australia.

ISBN hardcover 0 7134 3021 4
      paperback 0 7134 3022 2

Contents

List of Figures

List of Photographs

Acknowledgements

No book, least of all an overview, can be written without a great deal of help from a great number of people; that help I am delighted to acknowledge.

Firstly my thanks are due to my colleagues in the University of Canterbury, where the book was conceived and completed, and friends in the University of Cambridge, where it came into existence during a period of leave in 1972-3. The maps were drawn and many of the photographs prepared in the Department of Geography of the University of Canberbury, where too a difficult manuscript was transformed into an immaculate typescript. The origin of particular maps and pictures is acknowledged elsewhere and it remains to thank collectively the many individuals and institutions who helped in this respect. As this book was written in libraries and on the basis of their resources I most gladly acknowledge the expertise and tolerance of the many librarians who have helped me, particularly in Christchurch and Cambridge.

My teachers are now become too numerous to mention; nevertheless they deserve my thanks. Professor Gordon East has proved a most helpful editor, and two colleagues, Dr G. C. Wynn and Dr L. E. Richardson, geographer and historian respectively, undertook the arduous but essential task of reading a preliminary version and providing critical comment. Responsibility for failings and shortcomings is mine alone.

Finally I would wish to thank David Peat who whiled away my lunch hours, the campanologists of Cambridge and elsewhere with whom I enjoyed so many delightful evenings, Rachel-Mary who came as often as she could, and my many friends, relations and helpers who found themselves in some wise caught up with the making of this book.

Peter Perry

Christchurch, N.Z. 1974

For the Perrys and the Armitages

Introduction

The aim of this book is to acquaint students of nineteenth-century British history and twentieth-century British geography with the geography of nineteenth-century Britain. The book may interest my academic peers, but its particular concern is the needs of students in their last two years at school and their first and second years at university or college. With their requirements rather than with those characteristic of the research frontier I have tried to contend.

An assumption that some knowledge of the geography of nineteenth-century Britain is needed by the historian and the geographer makes no claim to originality. Rather it is to share the point of view of a number of notable historians, Macaulay, Trevelyan and Clapham for example, and of the doyen of British geographers, Clifford Darby. Darby has written that 'the foundations of geographical study lie in geomorphology and historical geography', and that these foundations exist to be built upon. My aim is then to underpin the larger structures of nineteenth-century history and twentieth-century geography. My experiences as a university teacher and my reading convince me that the methodological developments of the last quarter-century have neither removed the need for such underpinnings nor done very much to improve students' substantive or methodological grasp of these foundations. And at the risk of appearing arrogant I would thus claim to be taking part in the basic activity of every university, so succinctly expressed by Sir Alan Bullock in the phrase 'grappling with ignorance'.

I make no claim that this book is original scholarship (whatever that phrase may mean), but an organiser and arranger of 'other men's flowers' can scarcely avoid putting forward some of his own ideas, especially when he has hitherto worked in such areas as nineteenth-century population geography, transport geography, and, more recently and more extensively, agricultural geography. My involvement in these areas of research has, I think, facilitated and stimulated the operation of taking an overview which is the essence of this book. In parting company from the many academics who assert, by precept and practice, that the time is never ripe for taking such perspectives I would strongly assert that the research frontier is the proper place from which to view so rich a panorama. Whether or not the reader shares this point of view, or the substantive opinions put forward in the book itself, I can but hope that he enjoys reading it as much as I have enjoyed writing it.

1 Britain in 1800:
A Transitional Geography

Britain in 1800 was in the middle of that transition known to later generations as the Industrial Revolution[1]; a thinly peopled and primarily rural society on the periphery of Europe was becoming densely populated, urban and industrial, soon to occupy a lynch-pin role in the world economy. Many of these changes were conspicuous — canal building, road improvement, new cotton mills by the score in east Lancashire — but it would be a mistake to believe that these were the changes which captured the popular imagination at the start of the nineteenth century. The popular imagination was captured by Napoleon Bonaparte and his military success; a traveller through Britain could not fail to observe his impact on the landscape: army encampments, unusually active naval dockyards, defensive works such as the Royal Military Canal, even a surge of enclosure of open fields and wasteland brought about by wartime inflation and fears for the nation's food supply. Most of these changes were not of lasting importance; even those which were, enclosure for example, commonly extended beyond what could be sustained after the war. The fundamental changes were relatively inconspicuous — the population explosion, the establishment of factories, the widespread adoption of up-to-date farming methods. Moreover in certain sectors it is hard to see fundamental changes when allowance has been made for the effects of war; coalmining and wool manufacturing for example were progressing unspectacularly in established locations, by established methods and for established markets. If the economic, social and military situation favoured change it was not such as to bring about simultaneous or instantaneous revolution on a broad front. The political institutions of the period were certainly not such as directly to favour change for they reflected a vanished geography, rotten boroughs rather than manufacturing towns, and a traditional view of society in which the landed interest was pre-eminent over the urban or industrial. Where property rights were at stake Parliament acted, in regulating enclosure and canal and railway building for example; where they were not it was usually unconcerned, an attitude by no means unfavourable to the interests of the first generation of factory-building industrialists.

Early nineteenth-century Britain was then an institutionally conservative — its critics would probably have used stronger language, corrupt or rotten — society, but not so powerfully or deliberately so as effectively to restrain the forces of change, social, economic and geographic.

The methods and motives of those who brought about these changes were, in essence, the increase of private profit. They may have limited appeal in the 1970s, and indeed have recently been described as the 'unacceptable face of capitalism', but whether or not we approve we live in a world as much of their making as of ours. A survey of how the geography of Britain changed during the course of the nineteenth century must then point to the present; it must necessarily begin with a view of the geography of 1800. A comprehensive insight into this geography is impossible and like the surveyor's framework of bench marks any view is necessarily selective, providing nothing more than the basis from which important and accessible points may be picked out and described. The latter adjective is as important as the former, for there remain many lacunae in our knowledge of Britain at the start of the nineteenth century. Fragmented, partial and imperfect studies are the raw materials for an overview and they always will be, thus invalidating the commonest criticism of any attempt at scholarly synthesis — the limitations and shortcomings of what has already been done. The search for a final and authoritative historical geography of any period or place is sure to be as unending as the quest of the historical Jesus. The reward is not the finding but the seeking.

THE INCREASE OF POPULATION

In 1789 England and Wales had a population exceeding eight million, in 1815 exceeding 11 million; the population of Scotland grew from a million and a quarter in 1755 to exceed two million in 1821. These rates of increase are less spectacular than those of the Third World in the twentieth century, but

Figure 1. The population of Britain at the first (1801) census, and Ireland at the first (1821) census. (Persons per thousand acres: 1, 1600 and over; 2, 800-1599; 3, 400-799; 4, 200-399; 5, 100-199; 6, less than 99.) Note (i) axial belt from Thames to Mersey, (ii) high densities in East Anglia and the West of England, (iii) high and relatively uniform densities in Ireland. (Redrawn from Watson, J.W., and Sissons, J.B., *The British Isles: A Systematic Geography*, London, 1964, figure 29.)

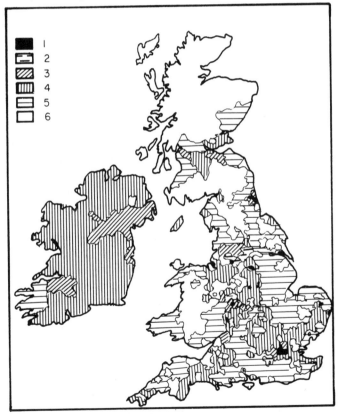

prior to the nineteenth century they had rarely been achieved and never sustained. The population geography of Britain at the start of the nineteenth century is not however merely a matter of spectacular numerical increase; geographical redistribution was both part of the phenomenon of increase and one of its causes. In fact much of the increase was concentrated in a few areas. In 1700 the most densely populated county in England, Worcestershire, had 141 persons per square mile; the least, Westmorland, 54 per square mile. Comparable figures in 1801 are 360 for Surrey and 55 for Westmorland. In some localities, notably but not exclusively in Scotland, depopulation on a modest scale had already begun in rural areas.

The general pattern of redistribution which was taking place eventually replaced the dominance of the lowland zone in general, East Anglia, London and the West Country in particular, by an axis of maximum population extending from London through the Midlands to Liverpool (figure 1). In 1800 this axis was very incomplete and interrupted and moreover there were other new areas of high density — the West Riding and central Scotland for example. The most rapid increase of population was to be found on the coalfield margins of the highland zone, where not only coal but also water power was most abundant, conspicuously in Lancashire. Much of this growth was as yet rural rather than urban: Liverpool and Manchester were growing fast, but even the newest cotton mills were as often as not in the countryside.

The increase of population in the cities and in the new industrial communities resulted on the one hand from migration, on the other from natural increase. The former process was, at this period, primarily one of local drift rather than long-distance movement; thus the labour force of Lancashire cotton and Black Country iron came from nearby rural areas, supplemented by a few Irish and Scots already willing to travel long distances in search of a job. These migrants were in turn replaced by people moving in from more remote rural communities. This kind of movement took place despite the existence of a Poor Law which inhibited mobility by providing relief only in the parish of 'settlement', in fact generally of origin. Such a model of population movement in the pre-railway age seems inherently likely and is supported by contemporary evidence; it does, however, leave a problematic loose end in some of the most remote and rural areas unless either a high level of natural increase in rural Britain at large or rural depopulation in distant parts is assumed. By comparison some much publicised movements, southern pauper children to northern mills for example, are unimportant. Early nineteenth-century population movement was in fact an unspectacular process.

The demographic mechanism underlying the increase of population and thus bearing on its redistribution is a more contentious issue, perhaps the most contentiously and continuously debated theme in British economic and social history. Did the large and rapid increase which took place — 14 per cent between 1801 and 1811 for example — result from fewer deaths or more births? In recent years a fall in the death rate has usually been regarded as the more important component, and it has been related by scholars to such diverse circumstances as food supply, clothing, housing, medical knowledge and even the Gin Acts. The issue is made even more difficult by uncertainty as to the timing and character of the increase before the 1801 census. In the 1950s renewed emphasis was given to the possible role of higher fertility in the second half of the eighteenth century as a major cause of increase. This reinterpretation has since been challenged, but it has served to emphasise the possibility of the operation of several spatially distinct mechanisms of increase. Higher fertility in urban areas than rural areas, at least in part a result of a different age-sex structure, has long been recognised as one of these. Secondly from late in the eighteenth century the death rate appears to have fallen faster in agricultural than in manufacturing communities, despite the age-sex structure — a consequence perhaps of a better diet and a healthier environment? An important new phenomenon is the recognition that the solution to the industrial and demographic problem may be largely geographical. Some such possible solutions have been examined: for example the long accepted view that the Speenhamland[2] system (the supplementation of the labourer's wage to subsistence level from the rates) encouraged larger families has been shown to be probably false. Others await attention — the higher wages of the farm labourer in the north by comparision with the south, the effects of 'open' and 'close' villages, the differences between the new manufacturing communities (youthful in their age-sex structure and with a market for child labour) and the old market and provincial towns.

Finally the geographical implications of rather localised population increase must be considered. More people had to be fed, clothed, housed and employed. Whether or not this was done badly or well, whether or not standards of living rose or fell, demands were made on particular resources and on the environment in general. They were answered as far as possible by old and new technologies or by straightforward expansion of existing practice. New mills were built, new mines were sunk, new land was brought into use, new landscapes and new environments were made. In many instances the rate of consumption of irreplaceable resources grew rapidly; coal and iron had been nibbled at in the eighteenth century, now they were gobbled up. It is scale, impact and timing which are the distinctive features of the Industrial Revolution and its demographic counterpart.

AGRICULTURE

A rapidly increasing population had to be fed, neither well fed, nor reliably fed, nor interestingly fed, by present-day standards, but at least kept alive and able to work. Fortunately a number of changes favouring agricultural improvement, particularly higher output per acre and per unit of capital, had been going on since at least the seventeenth century. Economic circumstances had been particularly favourable for these changes since about 1750. Wartime inflation, accompanied by a characteristic concern with the security of the nation's food supply and a run of adverse seasons, brought these changes to something of a climax early in the nineteenth century. This prosperity was for the farmer and landowner and was not shared by the labourer. Moreover a limited technology and wartime conditions generated a degree of distortion in patterns of land-use.

These changes were grafted onto an old established system, a mainly pastoral tradition in the highland north and west, and an arable tradition in the lowland south and east. These were linked by inter-regional movements of livestock (mostly on the hoof) and to some extent of grain. As there was no way of transporting perishable produce more than a few miles, and as bulky goods such as grain could only be moved cheaply over long distances by water, a degree of local and regional autonomy in food supply remained. But there were already well developed regional specialisations: orchards and hop-fields in Kent (handy for London markets); grazing in Leicestershire and the North Riding; store sheep and cattle breeding in Wales and Aberdeenshire respectively. Environmental constraints were as yet scarcely challenged, and thus since drainage techniques were superficial most heavy land was either indifferent permanent pasture or wheat-beans-fallow in rotation.

Enclosure or its absence was, however, of some importance in this respect. For example, where 'red lands' of the Oxfordshire Middle Lias were enclosed in the early nineteenth century the traditional open-field rotation of wheat-beans-barley-fallow gave way to the Norfolk four-course (wheat-turnips-barley-clover) followed by beans and oats.

Enclosure was only one among several determinants of farming practice. It was in its own final phase of efflorescence during the first two decades of the century, the characteristic change in the rural landscape, from open field or common to hedgerow and field. Farming paid well even as rents rose and often one-year tenancies ousted long leases. There was more concern over the nation's food supply than over security of tenure, and the response to these circumstances was to enclose and intensify. In Scotland the process contained a further dimension, the sometimes brutal transformation of peasant township to tenant farm and sheep run, a radical transformation of traditional society and its settlement pattern. The general social impact of enclosure is however debatable and has certainly at times been exaggerated; its impact on the landscape, made as it was over several centuries, remains evident.

Other opportunities for long-term agricultural investment remained limited; the technology of under-drainage barely existed, pedigree livestock were the fancy of the few rather than the mania of the many. The important contemporary development most easily overlooked was the general elevation of standards; thus Arthur Young observed in 1809 'a great change in their [the farmers'] ideas, knowledge and practice', although he went on to add a typical corrective — 'a great deal of ignorance and barbarity remains'[3]. Some of these changes related to the progress of manufacturing industry — grassing down in east Lancashire where there was an expanding market for butter, cheese, milk and meat for example — but they were also reported from remote and rural counties such as Pembrokeshire. The general economic (and military) situation more often favoured the breaking up of old grassland, such as the chalk downs, to provide for the forbears of the arable sheep, the Oxford and Hampshire Downs. Social changes also had their agricultural consequences, as when the Blackface sheep spread over the border from the Pennines to replace breeds suited to the old Scottish peasant townships.

Farm workers remained the largest occupational group in Britain. The labour force of the new industries came essentially from increase rather than from an exodus from the land. Agriculture was in fact intensive, but as yet unmechanised, and thus resembled industry in its demand for labour. However there is evidence of agricultural over-population, and thus individual impoverishment, in the rural south, where farm workers' wages were lower than in the north. Less rational and more localised was the mismatching of residence and workplace inherent in the existence of 'open' and 'close' villages, particularly in East Anglia and the East Midlands. In 'close' villages a single resident landowner restricted the number of houses and resident labourers to keep down the poor rates. Additional labour came from the fewer, often squalid, 'open' villages where landowners were too numerous to act so restrictively. In many cases this system operated at the cost of an exhaustingly long journey to work.

Farming was still Britain's basic industry in 1800 — only one-fifth of the population was urban — and it was prosperous in temporarily very favourable circumstances. On average the country was still just about self-sufficient, although beginning to depend on some imported inputs. How far this self-sufficiency was responsible for high prices, a pauperised labour force and a geographically rather irrational land-use pattern is arguable. These owed at least something to the war, and often served to mask less spectacular developments of more lasting significance.

INDUSTRY

To any traveller in Britain in 1800, particularly from overseas, the pace and scale of industrial growth must have seemed astonishing. His attention would probably been drawn to cotton and iron in particular, to the most spectacular and most basic of industries, but he could scarcely fail to notice more localised examples, non-ferrous metals in the Swansea valley, chemicals at Glasgow, not least for the environmental devastation they were causing. Even industries which were losing ground on a relative scale, wool for example, were generally growing and prosperous in war conditions. Moreover the war brought new industries which were to prove long-lasting to some towns, bootmaking to Leicester for example.

Coal was not the most evidently expanding industry in 1800; it had not attained the importance of its late nineteenth-century Golden Age of steam ships, steam railways, steam-driven machinery and huge export markets. Nevertheless coal was already a common form of domestic heating, integral to iron-making, and exercising a growing locational power over manufacturing industry in general through the steam engine, although it had not yet eliminated water power as a motive force and locational factor. By a fortunate chance coal and water power were often geographically coincident, as on the Pennine margins.

Coal output probably exceeded ten million tons per annum by 1800. Northumberland and Durham produced a third of the nation's coal and the antiquity of the industry in this area and its role as London's supplier of 'sea coal' ensured that it received a great deal of notice. A larger share of output, perhaps two-fifths, came from the pits of Lancashire, Yorkshire and the Midlands, and was destined for less conspicuous local industrial and domestic use. Scotland, Wales, Cumberland and the Somerset-Bristol field were the other main producers.

Technologically the industry was starting to move from the primitive to the sophisticated. Most pits were shallow and in the form of a bell[4], and therefore shortlived; but in Cumberland a depth of nearly 1,000 feet had been reached. There were more and more large enterprises such as the Lowther mine, employing 200 men in 1811, a development owing much to the increased use of underground tramways. These were almost as important to the growth of the industry as the more obvious device of the surface tramway. Coalmining remained a dangerous job, but the tramway and the northward spread of longwall working to replace 'bord and pillar'[5] ensured increased productivity. The typical colliery was a group of several pits together with a larger number of abandoned workings, often in a semi-rural setting and sometimes by 1800 served by a canal. Most coalfields were remote from the established centres of population and were themselves less densely populated than the manufacturing areas. Coalmining was labour-intensive, but the population of Durham and Northumberland in 1801 was less than half that of Lancashire. Salford Hundred (Manchester excluded) had more people than either county. There was however some degree of association with coal-consuming industry: integrated coal and iron industries operated in Wales and Scotland, coalpits were owned by Cheshire salt manufacturers. On the other hand coal remained prohibitively expensive in some inland areas, in the south of England in particular. As the eighteenth century gave place to the nineteenth the adult collier found his work less arduous, his earnings higher and his domestic circumstances more civilised[6]. The industry grew, but its most rapid growth awaited new markets, new technologies, new means of transportation (plate 1).

Cotton was something of a 'boom and bust' industry in the early nineteenth century — expansion was rapid but erratic. Nevertheless its proportionate contribution to the gross national product doubled in the first decade of the century. Like coal it was an industry of the upland margins, not only in and around east Lancashire, already its principal locale, but also in Scotland, the East Midlands and more widely. Water power rather than coal was the principal locational force in the early years of factory cotton spinning between about 1780 and 1810; during this period cotton manufacturers were active in converting old water mills as well as in building new ones. The good fortune of the country around Manchester was its endowment with coal as well as water. By 1800 spinning was well on course to become an exclusively factory activity. Weaving remained largely domestic, widely dispersed within the spinning area, and as yet prosperous. Factory spinning made for cheap and plentiful yarn, but factory weaving was faced with technical problems. The geographical separation of spinning and weaving, south and north of Rossendale, had not yet begun, but more localised specialisation was already evident — fine spinning in Bolton, calicoes in Blackburn, muslin on Clydeside. Raw materials were the particular concern of Liverpool as an importer and of the canals as distributors.

Cotton has always been regarded as the epitome of the early phase of the Industrial Revolution in particular. The rapid growth of a large-scale industry was both spectacular and of major economic significance. Largely as a result the population of Manchester township grew from 22,481 in 1774 to 70,409 in 1801, and of the whole parish from 41,032 to 102,300. New settlements, created by the industry, grew even more rapidly around the water wheels or steam engines of the spinning mills. The evident dynamism of the rising industry attracted further investment, the motive force of its further growth and more extensive geographical impact.

The eighteenth-century iron industry was *par excellence* the industry of transformed technology. Some time in the early eighteenth century Abraham Darby made iron with coke, a relatively slowly adopted innovation; the puddling process[7] for wrought iron manufacture was developed in the 1780s and much more speedily taken up. Moreover the coalfields provided not only the fuel and reducing agent but also the black-band ores, the industry's principal raw material until the second half of the nineteenth century. It is thus no surprise that the Northumberland and Durham coalfield, ill-endowed with such ores, saw the most meagre development of the industry at this date.

New technology was one cause of the rapid growth of the iron industry in the years around 1800. The Napoleonic war boosted one traditional market, the increased popularity of the steam engine another. It appears that there was an approximately fourfold increase in output between the late 1780s and 1806, when about a quarter of a million tons was produced. The West midlands and South Wales accounted for two-thirds of this, already, as has been noted, in some degree of integration with mining. Likewise the characteristic location was as yet semi-rural on the margin of the uplands. Within the West Midlands the main centre of production was already moving to Staffordshire from the relative remoteness and inaccessibility of Shropshire; Scotland and the West Riding were the other main areas of production but as yet they were growing less rapidly than the major centres. At the other extreme the Weald, the traditional centre of English iron-making, ceased to produce at some date between 1796, when 173 tons were made, and 1806. The industry had moved to coal.

It is impossible to go on to examine the impact of the Industrial Revolution on every industry, not least because of the continuing importance of domestic manufacturing. The woollen industry, for several centuries pre-eminent among Britain's manufactures, was still largely domestic in the West Riding, Norfolk and the West of England, its three main centres. So also were the Bridport rope and net industry, pin and needle making at Gloucester and Redditch for example. The pace and extent to which these activities passed to the factory — and net-making remains partly domestic — depended on the chances of location, technical change and entrepreneurial activity. Among the last to fall were some that might be regarded as family activities rather than domestic industry — baking and garment-making for example — and here too an element of home activity has survived. The limited evidence suggests what might be expected, that this domestic, and at times subsistence, element in the economy was more marked and persistent in the highland zone of northern and western Britain than in the lowland south and east, ironically in the same area as the earliest factory triumphs. At the same time there were industries which though small in scale and widely dispersed were, for technical reasons, rarely domestic — flour-milling (albeit the mill was often attached to a house) and paper-making for example.

MOBILITY

For most of the inhabitants of Britain at the start of the nineteenth century transport and movement meant walking. They could afford no other way, and in many instances lived off the beaten track of even the humblest carrier's cart. The technology as well as the finance of mass transportation lay in the future, coastal shipping to some degree excepted. Thus people walked: to work, to seek a wife, to sell their produce or their labour. The chapman or pedlar, his goods on his back or his packhorse, carried on a substantial part of the country's retail trade, while the pedestrian drover managed an important part of its food supply — Welsh cattle[8] and, less spectacularly if more chaotically, poultry from the home counties to London, for example. Pedestrian power was even used to propel narrow boats through canal tunnels.

The roads and lanes used by these walkers, by coach, by cart, and by horseman, were generally in an unsatisfactory state. Neither the problems of road management and finance nor those or road construction had been solved. Most roads were cared for — inasmuch as this took place at all — by the parishes through which they passed; the task was reluctantly undertaken and ineffectively executed. The chances were that the turnpike trusts, responsible for about one-fifth of the mileage, would act more energetically but still with limited expertise. Only Metcalfe among the great trinity of English road builders had carried out much work by 1800; the full fruition of his ideas, and those of Macadam and Telford, belongs to the succeeding generation. The quality of the road surface in 1800 was more likely to reflect available raw materials, a matter of geology, and the energy and affluence of those charged with its care, than technological expertise. Only a few wealthy bodies, the City of London for example, could afford to import exotic durables such as Purbeck stone for mere road making.

Yet despite these problems the roads had improved since 1750. More legislation relating to roads passed through Parliament, including a General Turnpike Act in 1773, and more traffic passed along the roads. Moreover traffic moved faster, the surest sign of better conditions,, not least because of work to ease gradients. Edinburgh had been 10-12 days from London in 1754; it was four days by 1776. The roads were generally at their best near the towns (more money counting for more than more traffic), in the summer, and off the clays; winter traffic was often discouraged and in such areas as the Weald might find it extremely difficult to move anyway. In these circumstances it is scarcely surprising that both road and road improvement were expensive. Indeed some turnpike trusts were financially unsound before the railways were built. The passenger paid a particularly high price for speed: inside fares on fast coaches were of the order of fourpence to fivepence a mile. By comparison with the fast coach, freight haulage by road was a long-established business, although by 1800 canal competition had reduced its role to that of a feeder in some areas. Thus Pickford, one of the major carriers, gradually transferred his London base to the City Wharf from 1806.

The canal network was essentially a late eighteenth-century creation, and by 1800 the Thames, the Severn, the Mersey and the Humber were connected via the Midlands. The Pennines and the Thames-Severn watershed were each crossed by three canals early in the nineteenth century. Quicker and more reliable than road haulage, canal carriage was also very much cheaper; bulky goods of low value such as bricks and grain were carried at one quarter to one half the cost of road transport. Not surprisingly the canals soon handled all traffic of this kind in the areas they served, depending however on the horse and cart for the first and/or last stage of distribution. By comparison passenger traffic was never of much importance; this passed directly from coach or coastal shipping to the railway.

The canal companies provided the waterway and its services; they were rarely carriers. A diversity of canal companies meant a diversity of dimensions, an obstacle to efficient nationwide use. Moreover many canals were built extremely slowly. Only those built cheaply and at an early date were generally profitable, particularly those in industrial districts. Rural canals, the reputedly trunk routes across such watersheds as the Cotswolds, paid poorly if at all. But the canal investor was not always primarily seeking a dividend. He might be wishing to market his produce — as in the case of the Glamorgan Canal for example, to export his coal. Outside the Midlands and the neighbourhood of the four major estuaries the canal network was as fragmentary as it was unprofitable; much of Britain was remote from the canals and their influence. Where they were built they were a conspicuously new and notably persistent feature in landscape and economy.

Britain's maritime trade passed through a very large number of ports, some of them very small and handling no more than two or three cargoes of, say, coal or timber a year. Not only were there numerous small ports but also small vessels; a great deal of coastwise trade was carried on in vessels of no more than ten tons. Even the important Newfoundland trade carried on across the stormy North Atlantic involved numerous vessels of no more than 100 tons. The steamer was still an idea or a toy.

By common consent the coal trade, particularly between London and the Tyne, was the most important part of the coastwise trade, employing a greater tonnage than the whole overseas trade. 'Sea coal' was cheap on the coast but increasingly expensive inland. Much of the overseas trade was 'protected', to the British West Indies and British North America for example, and some of it was still monopolistic and quasi-military such as that of the East India Company. London and Liverpool were the major ports and by 1800 the latter had already begun to build its dock system; London followed in the first decade of the nineteenth century. At the same time remote, ancient, and nationally unimportant harbour works such as the Cobb at Lyme Regis could still look to government aid for major repairs even if at least some of its users were at the same time defrauding the government of revenue by smuggling.

PATTERNS OF SETTLEMENT

Population increase and redistribution necessarily brought about a new geography of settlement, but these were not the only forces for change in this context. Enclosure usually led to some dispersal of settlement in the lowland zone, and the new farmhouses which were built in the process often reflected the wider availability of brick and the decay of vernacular tradition in areas served by the canals. In the highland zone enclosure sometimes meant dispossession and depopulation rather than dispersal. In other respects established patterns survived, the tacit acceptance of a low standard of housing for the mass of the population for example. The one-room cottage was commonplace in Scotland and by no means unknown in England and Wales in 1800.

If rural settlement was to some degree controlled and planned the typical industrial settlement of 1800 sprawled unorganisedly around its parent mill or forge and only occasionally did an owner[9] give form and shape to the domestic part of the new industrial landscape. Sometimes, as at Oldham, the enclosure of waste land was intimately associated with new urban growth. In many instances a rural setting redeemed these communities, at least during their formative years, from the consequences of unplanned and rapid growth, but it could not for ever stave off the effects of poor building methods, non-existent drainage and sewerage, unpaved and unlit roads and lanes. Industrialisation created not only 'scores of little colonies centred on the new mills'[10] but new suburbs or simply a higher density of population in existing towns. These latter provided some of the worst living conditions. Nottingham for one was hemmed in by open fields controlled by intransigent burgesses and by parks owned by noble but inflexible lords. Where 10,000 people had lived in 1739 there were nearly 30,000 in 1801, workers in lace and knitwear manufacture, inhabitants of 'a chequerboard of mean streets, alleyways and courts, and a byeword for filth and misery beyond belief'.[11] Ironically some 'close' villages no more than a few miles from Nottingham were actually losing population during this period. Country towns had their alleyways and courts too but they rarely had to face such pressures as the manufacturing communities, and for a few wartime agricultural prosperity brought about a rebuilding or a face-lift.

The settlement geography of 1800 is then a geography of heightened contrasts, of the emergence of new communities and new forms of settlement on the margins of the uplands, and of an initial and transient phase of urbanisation not repeated until the 1920s. New materials from hitherto inaccessible sources competed with the local and traditional in areas opened up by the canals. A continuance of dispersion characterised the lowland zone, incipient depopulation the heart of highland zone.

ENVIRONMENTAL IMPACT

What kind of impact were the British making — and had they made — on their environment in 1800? Thousands of years of occupation even at low, although slowly increasing, population densities had made demands upon resources and had organised their use. Thus the last wave of enclosure was but one stage in a continuous and continuing process of bringing most of Britain into pastoral or agricultural occupation. Already there was a shortage of timber and demands on non-renewable resources such as coal and iron had increased sharply during the eighteenth century. The methods used to extract these resources were often very damaging to the environment, the shallow 'bell' coalpit for example, where a high risk of subsidence was associated with numerous workings over a wide area to obtain a little coal. This was not only a matter of the rights of property and of limited technology but of a failure fully to apprehend the nature of the resource. New factories were less directly damaging, adding to the already numerous dams and weirs and increasing coal consumption, creating concentrations of houses and their refuse; their most distinctive form of pollution was associated with bleaching and dyeing and appears not to have become a severe problem by 1800.

Atmospheric pollution, the concentration of domestic and industrial chimneys, and river pollution, the use of running water for rubbish disposal, were established situations rather than new problems. Novelty was to be found in the increasing extent and concentration and new locations of such activity. Comment — and opposition — was reserved for the new noxious industries, the Swansea valley copper works for example. There in 1804 'the columns of smoke from the different manufactories contribute to make Swansea if not unwholesome a very disagreeable place of residence'.[12] The major problems lay in the future: while Rennie calculated that in 1808 the Thames received 800,000 tons of mud and rubbish a year from London and its inhabitants, a marked deterioration and a public concern culminated only in the 'great stink' of 1858.[13]

Early nineteenth-century society took dirt for granted. It was part of the human condition, an inevitable accompaniment of industrialisation and urbanisation, and its role in disease was as yet little understood. Although the water closet was patented in 1775 and 1778, the sanitary revolution is essentially a feature of the nineteenth century. Absence of comment does not imply absence of concern or of problems, but the evidence suggests that mismanagement of the environment had as yet produced problems only for a few people and in a few areas. That a large number of people were poorly housed was to some degree a matter for regret, but as this had always been so, it scarcely called for urgent action. When Blake wrote of 'dark satanic mills'[14] early in the nineteenth century he symbolised a likely future rather than an actual present.

REGIONAL PATTERNS

As important a question as that of environmental impact is that of regional patterns, the regional geography of Britain. In 1800 most people were still living out their lives within narrow spatial limits, the farm, the village, the occasional — perhaps annual — visit to the market town. The world of the factory worker — mill, terrace and 'tommy shop'[15] — was if anything even more limited than that of his country cousin. The Napoleonic War, like all wars, had jerked a number of men out of this constrained geographical context, but only temporarily, and most people lived out their lives within narrow spatial limits.

Functional regions on a larger scale existed within the economy, indeed for some purposes, the rearing and fattening of cattle for example, Britain as a whole acted as such. The spatial association and interdigitation of coal, iron and iron-using manufactures in the West Midlands and the existence of a concentration of paper manufacturing around London are examples of more localised functional regions. Each port possessed its hinterland, distorted from geometrical simplicity by such circumstances as topography, turnpike gates, and harbour dues. Likewise the county and the county town provided a functional region and a focus for the social life of the middle and upper classes; a small number of specially or fortuitously favoured towns such as Bath and Brighton fulfilled a similar national role.

Superimposed upon this pattern or system of functional regions was one of broad regional differences. The most basic of these, the highland zone and the lowland zone, is as old as the human occupation of Britain; to some degree it was becoming muted by 1800 as new farming methods spread into the highland zone and such processes as enclosure re-organised settlement patterns. But as these old differences diminished so new dichotomies emerged, in the wages and productivity of agricultural labour between north and south, in the character and forms of urban life between the old provincial towns and the new factory communities, in the relationship between population increase and employment opportunity in town and country. Benjamin Disraeli the novelist and later prime minister used the phrase 'the two nations' to summarise the situation as it had developed by 1845, comparing the rich and the poor;[16]

the geographer may prefer to think of three, juxtaposing the new manufacturing and mining centres of the upland margins — the new Britain of 1800 — with either highland zone and lowland zone, or with town and country (plates 2 and 3), and thus comparing the dynamo and mainspring of nineteenth-century geographical change with sharply contrasted conservative forces.

NOTES

1 The phrase was coined not by contemporary observers but by Arnold Toynbee in his Oxford lectures, published after his death in 1883.
2 So called because it was adopted, though not invented, by the Berkshire magistrates, meeting at the Pelican Inn, Speenhamland, a suburb of Newbury, in 1795. It was widely adopted in the south and regarded by contemporaries as a cause of population increase.
3 Young, A., *General View of the Agriculture of Oxfordshire*, London, (revised edition) 1813, p.35.
4 That is, their cross-section approximated to that of a bell, with a short vertical shaft for access.
5 'Bord and pillar' left coal standing as supports between the workings and thus removed less than half of the available coal; 'longwall' removed all available coal. For detailed descriptions see Ashton, T.S. and Sykes, J., *The Coal Industry of the Eighteenth Century*, Manchester, (2nd edition) 1964, pp. 14-32.
6 Ashton, T.S., and Sykes, J., *The Coal Industry of the Eighteenth Century*, Manchester, (2nd edition) 1964, p. 174.
7 This allowed wrought iron to be made with coal instead of the much more expensive charcoal.
8 An interesting survey of four centuries of this trade is Skeel, C., 'The cattle trade between Wales and England from the fifteenth to the nineteenth centuries', *Transactions of the Royal Historical Society*, series 4, vol. 9, 1926, pp. 135-55.
9 Robert Owen (1771-1858) took over New Lanark mills in 1800 where he built a model village and schools, limiting child labour, and mixing a degree of socialism with a deal of

paternalism.

10 Millward, R., *Lancashire: an illustrated essay on the History of the landscape*, London, 1955, p. 78.

11 Chambers, J.D., *Modern Nottingham in the Making*, Nottingham, 1945, p. 6.

12 Hilton, K.J. (ed.), *The Lower Swansea Valley Project*, London, 1967, p. 26.

13 Ehrlich, B., *London on the Thames*, London, 1968, pp. 32-4. One result of the 'great stink' was the *Report of the Select Committee on the River Thames*, 1858.

14 William Blake in the introductory lines to his poem 'Milton' written between 1800 and 1804. It is often, and incorrectly, referred to as 'Jerusalem'.

15 Because mills and mines were commonly isolated and worked long hours, their owners often ran shops to provide for their employees' needs. To the unscrupulous these 'tommy shops' were a marvellous opportunity for sharp practice and profiteering — see Benjamin Disraeli, *Sybil or the Two Nations*, 1845, ch. 3. The practice was outlawed by the Truck Acts of 1831 and 1887.

16 Benjamin Disraeli, *Sybil or the Two Nations*, 1845. The novel is set in the late 1830s, in part in a mining community. It contains not only brilliant and cogent economic and social criticism, but much sound historical geography.

FURTHER READING

Agriculture, Board of, *The Agricultural State of the Kingdom*, London, 1816 (reprinted, with an introduction by G.E. Mingay, Bath, 1970).

Aiken, J., *A Description of the Country from Thirty to Forty Miles Round Manchester*, London, 1795 (reprinted Newton Abbot, 1968).

Armstrong, W.A., 'La population de l'Angleterre et du pays de Galles, 1789-1815', *Annales de Démographie Historique*, 1965, pp. 31-38.

Ashton, T.S., and Sykes, J., *The Coal Industry of the Eighteenth Century*, Manchester, (2nd edition) 1964.

Clapham, Sir J.H., *An Economic History of Modern Britain:*

Volume 1 The Early Railway Age 1820-1850, Cambridge, 1926 (Book 1, 'Britain on the Eve of the Railway Age')

Crump, W.B., (ed.), *The Leeds woollen industry 1780-1820*, Leeds, Thoresby Society, volume 32, 1931.

Edwards, M.M., *The Growth of the British Cotton Trade 1780-1815*, Manchester, 1967.

Gleave, M.B., 'Dispersed and nucleated settlement in the Yorkshire Wolds 1770-1850', *Institute of British Geographers: Transactions and Papers*, No. 30, 1962, pp. 105-18.

Halfpenny, E., '"Pickfords": expansion and crisis in the early nineteenth century', *Business History*, vol. 1, 1959, pp. 115-25.

Lambert, A.M., 'The agriculture of Oxfordshire at the end of the eighteenth century.' *Agricultural History*, vol. 29(1), 1955, pp. 31-8.

2 People and Place:
The Geography of Population and Settlement

Population growth and productivity increase were the essence and the dynamic of Britain's experience in the nineteenth century. The evaluation is that of an historian, Kitson Clark,[1] the topics are as legitimately a workplace for the geographer and are the concern of the greater part of this book. Both population growth and productivity increase were accompanied by geographical redistribution and were subject to geographical constraints. This chapter considers the increase of population and then the resultant reorganisation of patterns of settlement, possibly the more basic and certainly the more closely defined of these two major themes.

Britain's first census took place in 1801 (fig. 1, p. 3) and was repeated, with generally increasing accuracy and detail, every ten years. The relatively bald and simple 1801 enumeration took place in the middle of the population explosion and is thus an inappropriate starting point for discussion of the mechanics and implications of that explosion.[2] More often the period from about 1750 to 1830 is considered as something of a unity, at least in part because better demographic data become available after the latter date, an effective system of registration of births, marriages and deaths in 1837, the census enumerators' books in 1841, and a particularly detailed census in 1851.

Great Britain's population of 10.5 million in 1801 reached 37 million by 1901. The country had also provided large numbers of emigrants, more than 120,000 per annum in peak years as early as mid-century. Population increase was more rapid in earlier decades of the century and in urban areas. The highest rate of overall increase from one census to the next was achieved between 1811 and 1821 and it was also during this decade that rural increase was at a maximum. For the largest towns, those with more than 20,000 people, the maximum rate of increase was reached only in the decade 1831-1841 but their lower rates of increase earlier in the century were still greater than rates of increase in rural areas at this date. As early as the decade 1841-1851 one English, three Welsh, and eight Scottish counties recorded a decrease of population. By 1851 more than half the population lived in towns (boroughs or places with more than 2000 people); by 1901 nearly four-fifths lived in boroughs or urban districts, an almost exact reversal of the 1801 situation. London had one million people in 1801, seven million in 1901; even at the start of the nineteenth century people were moving out from the city centre to rural or surburban Paddington and Poplar, and a 'census' taken in 1866 revealed that the City had twice as many commuters as residents.

Other cities and towns grew as spectacularly, mining and manufacturing centres and ports in particular. Small towns provide the most striking instances: Barry had a population of 100 in 1881, of 13,000 ten years later. Although rural depopulation was widespread in the second half of the century few counties had a smaller population in 1901 than 1801, and over wide areas population density had altered remarkably little. Great changes were confined to certain small — and discontinuous — areas of Britain. The rapid growth of London and Lancashire in the first half of the century so far outstripped the experience of other areas that even relatively rapidly industrialising counties such as Derbyshire, Nottinghamshire, and Leicestershire were increasing in population at a rate less than the national average during this period. In the second half of the century 30 per cent of all registration districts (certainly a smaller proportion of total area) increased in population at a rate faster than the national average. Nevertheless this high degree of localisation was part of a broad redistribution of population away from the ancient pre-eminence of the rural lowland zone towards the dominance of London and the new manufacturing and mining communities of the Midlands, the North of England, Wales and Scotland.

MECHANISMS OF GROWTH

Britain's population increased throughout the nineteenth century because the level of fertility remained higher than the level of mortality. This situation came into existence before 1800 and was sustained beyond 1900, although during the course of the century the difference between the two diminished. Moreover where mortality had been diminishing more rapidly than fertility, the reverse of this situation came to prevail. In neither instance did major changes occur early in the century; the nationwide decline in crude and standardised death rates first appears in the 1860s, for the very young and the old 20 years later. The control of infant mortality is in fact essentially a twentieth-century phenomenon: in the 1840s 72 children per 1,000 died in their first five years, in the 1890s 63, by the 1930s 20. The same is true of fertility; there were 137 births per 1,000 women of childbearing age in the 1840s, 123 in the 1890s — realisation of the socio-economic advantages of a smaller family had as yet had little effect — less than 80 in the late 1930s.

These changes during the nineteenth century were primarily the result of an improved environment rather than of better medical care. The diminishing impact of tuberculosis, responsible for perhaps half the reduction of the death rate between 1851 and 1901, was a matter not of drugs and hospitals but of diet and housing. Typhoid and cholera retreated in the face of drains and a safe water supply. More fortuitously the virulence of scarlet fever sharply diminished from a peak in the 1860s. By comparison the new antiseptic surgery and the old methods of smallpox control, effective though they were, had little significance (recent research ranks therapeutic advance only fourth as a factor in nineteenth-century mortality decline, after food, sanitation and the lessened virulence of scarlet fever). The eventual decline in fertility was more a matter of attitude than of technical progress; crude but effective contraceptive methods had been known and used, where it was felt they were needed, for centuries. In the nineteenth-century context some commentators on changing fertility have emphasised a shifting of the economic balance in favour of smaller families as child labour was restricted and educational compulsion extended; others have favoured a broader explanation embracing an extension of middle class attitudes and aspirations through a widening sector of the population as well as public, and at times highly publicised, debate on new contraceptive methods late in the century.

All of these circumstances, the virulence of scarlet fever excepted, contained a geographical component. The reliability of sewage disposal, the quality of the water supply, the level of real wages — and thus the quality of clothing, food and housing — varied from place to place even within a single industry or community. Likewise children were outlawed from the mines half a century before the 'part timer'[2] ceased to contribute to the farm labour force and the parental purse. The figures for life expectancy (in 1837) given below are thus scarcely surprising:

	Average age at death	
	Manchester	Rutland
Professions and gentry	38	52
Tradesmen and farmers	20	41
Mechanics and labourers	17	38

What is surprising is that so little work has been done on these differences and their consequences. It seems likely that through most of the century and for most people rural Britain was healthier than urban, bearing in mind however that there was a persistent although diminishing industrial element in the rural economy. The farmworker enjoyed probably a healthier workplace and a lower risk of unemployment, possibly the freshest food but certainly the lowest wages; his children remained an economic asset longer than in any other occupation. How far was this the basis of the ability of rural areas to supply part of the nineteenth-century urban labour force, and what was the complementary role of natural increase in urban growth and eventual urban dominance?

MIGRATION AND INCREASE

The concentration of nineteenth-century population increase, whatever its origins, into a small number of areas — the making of the first conurbations — thus raises the question how far their growth was self-sustaining or continuously dependent on migration? The evident existence of migration, the unhealthy urban environment, and perhaps the intrinsic appeal of the topic, have tended to create an emphasis on migration: recent research indicates the pre-eminence of natural increase — the cities were after all communities of young adults — while acknowledging the role of population movement.

For the period of 1801-1831, that of the first four censuses, only estimates of the respective roles of natural increase and migration are possible. These have been made by Deane and Cole (figures 2-4) who concluded that the industrial and commercial counties owed twice as much of their growth to natural increase as to in-migration. Only London (Surrey and

Figure 2. Estimated natural population increase as a percentage of total population increase in England (by counties) and Wales 1801-31: 1, more tnan 200%; 2, 150%-200%; 3, 100%-150%; 4, 50%-100%; 5, less than 50%. (Deane, P., and Cole, W.A., *British Economic Growth 1688-1959*, Cambridge, 1962, drawn from table 25.)

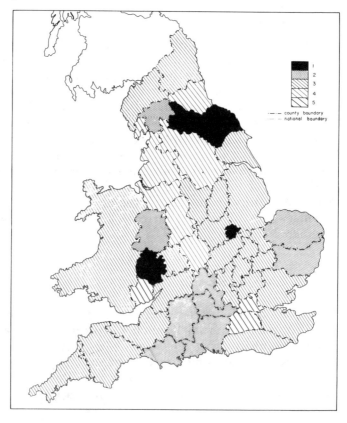

Middlesex) owed more than half its increase to migration, and both its excess of births over deaths and its demographic magnetism were diminishing by comparison with the previous century. Among other major areas of population increase Lancashire owed little more than a quarter of its increase to migration and Warwickshire was in a similar position; in Staffordshire and the West Riding the migrant's role was minimal. This latter contrast may however be a statistical accident, as a serious limitation of census-based migration studies for this period is that they necessarily define migration in terms of crossing a county boundary. The main centrés of population in Lancashire and Warwickshire, Manchester and Birmingham, are, like London, much closer to the county

Figure 3. Migration and natural increase (rates per thousand) in England (by counties) and Wales, 1801-30. (Drawn from same source as figure 2, table 26.)

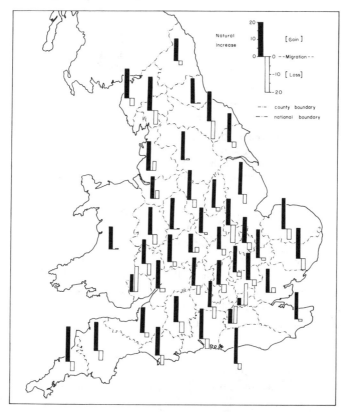

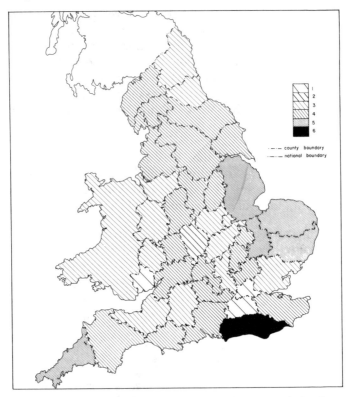

Figure 4. Differences between average birth rates and death rates
(b.r. — d.r.) in England (by counties) and Wales, 1801-30: 1, less
than 10.0; 2, 10.0-12.5; 3, 12.5-15.0; 4, 15.0-17.5; 5, 17.5-20.0; 6,
more than 20.0 (Drawn from same source as figure 2, table 29.)

boundary than their peers in Yorkshire and Staffordshire. But
there exists the possibility that earlier urbanisation and a less
dispersed industrial population in the first two counties, in fact
a closer resemblance to London, accounted for their greater
dependence on in-migration. Wide variations in birth and death
rates from county to county are generally evident at this period,
but on the whole a fall in death rates is apparent in London and
rural counties, the cumulative impact of two centuries of
agricultural advance. A rise in birth rates accounts for the
increasing population of mining and manufacturing counties.

Work on the period after 1831, notably by Cairncross,
Lawton, Fiedlander and Welton, rests on a more sophisticated

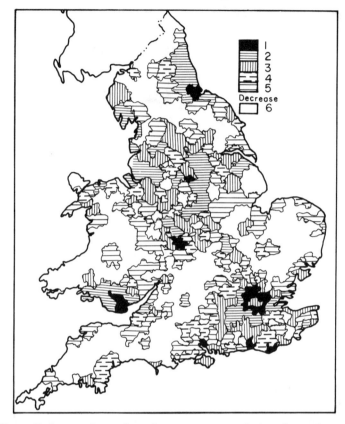

Figure 5. Summations of total percentage population change in each census decade (by registration district), England and Wales, 1851-1911: 1, 200 and over; 2, 100-200; 3, 50-100; 4, 25-50; 5, 0-25; 6, decrease. (Redrawn from Lawton, R., 'Rural depopulation in nineteenth century England', in Steel, R.W., and Lawton, R., *Liverpool Essays in Geography*, Liverpool, 1967, p.236.)

statistical base (figures 5-7). Throughout the middle decades of the century a relatively steady stream of migrants headed for the towns, southern as well as northern. In the 1880s this flow, to the northern towns in particular, was sharply checked, despite the existence of agricultural depression. Reputed, possibly real, industrial depression converted migrants to emigrants and only the south coast resorts retained an internal magnetism. This trend was reversed in the 1890s but was resumed after 1900. The demographic attraction of particular

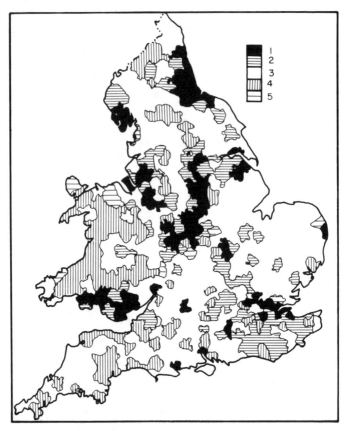

Figure 6. Summations of percentage natural change (i.e. balance of births and deaths) in each census decade (by registration district), England and Wales, 1851-1911: 1, 100 and over; 2, 80-100; 3, 60-80; 4, 40-60; 5, less than 40. (Redrawn from same source as figure 5, p.238.)

coalfields varied from decade to decade, but their overall role was consistently to attract about 100,000 migrants per decade, and to a greater extent than the manufacturing towns they were pre-eminently areas of high natural increase. Dependence on migration for growth was associated particularly with the early stages of rapid industrial urbanisation — Middlesborough and Merthyr Tydfil, boom towns of the middle and early decades of the century respectively, are good examples. In some rural areas out-migration had reduced fertility as early as the 1860s, but

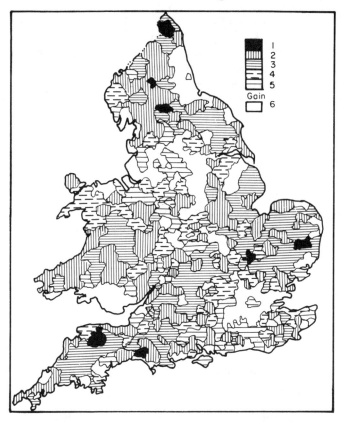

Figure 7. Summations of percentage net migrational loss (i.e. balance of natural and total change) in each census decade (by registration district), England and Wales, 1851-1911: 1, 100 and over; 2, 75-100; 3, 50-75; 4, 25-50; 5, 0-25; 6, gain. (Redrawn from same source as figure 5, p.240.)

relatively low mortality and large families generally sustained a steady outflow with but localised absolute depopulation. Lawton's maps (figures 5-7) for the period 1851-1911 aptly summarise the situation: in Cairncross's words 'the north of England triumphed over the south mainly by superior fertility (and not, as we used to be taught, by attracting migrants). In seventy years the north gained three more inhabitants for every two added to the population of the south'.[3] Marriage triumphed over mobility. A triumph extending back beyond the beginning of the century but barely sustained to its end.

The relative importance of migration and natural increase in the changing geography of the Scottish population has been less thoroughly analysed than the situation in England and Wales. While in the broad sense Scottish socio-economic development in the nineteenth century paralleled that south of the border, three factors suggest that migration was proportionately more important to the north. Not only was there an established tradition of out-migration from densely populated and technically primitive farming districts in the Highlands and Islands, but there was also a rather higher degree of geographical localisation of economic and demographic growth, particularly in the Clyde Valley, and a Poor Law slightly more favourable to movement. Local statisticians were generally convinced of the importance of migration — of late eighteenth-century Greenock it was said that one could 'walk from one end of the town to the other . . . without hearing a word of any language but Gaelic'.[4] It remains for present-day scholars to prove or disprove their contention.

MECHANISMS OF MOVEMENT

The propensity to migrate like the propensity to increase possessed a distinctive geography. Migration is a geographical phenomenon in a second sense — how far? in what direction? — which requires as much attention as the matter of differences in its regional impact.

Ravenstein's work on migration during the decade 1871-1881, published in 1885, demonstrated that movement took place more often in short steps than in large leaps (plate 4), and that a wave or ripple motion of this kind served to bring people from country to city. Such movement took place up the hierarchy of settlement, from farm to hamlet, hamlet to village, village to town, town to city. It was generated on the one hand by the attractive force of the towns and cities — city lights and city wages — and by a degree of rural over-population indicated by very low wages for example. It is also possible that it owed something to the retreat of cultivation — and population — from marginal areas during the prolonged depression after 1815. Ravenstein's model has been substantially confirmed by subsequent scholarship, albeit with strictures relating to differences in county size, and is regarded as the norm not only for the nineteenth but for earlier centuries. It can scarcely be said to have been rigorously tested; this may in fact be impossible, and

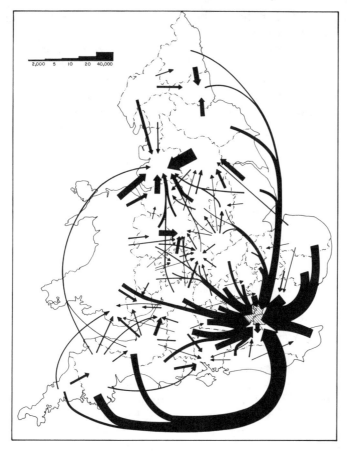

Figure 8. Net numbers of persons migrating between counties, 1861 census. (Redrawn from Smith, C.T., 'The movement of population in England and Wales in 1851 and 1861', *Geographical Journal*, Vol. 117, 1951, p.206.)

local and nationwide studies for the decade 1851-1861 have indicated its limitations (figure 8). Certainly in the second half of the century direct long-distance movement became common-place for skilled workmen and the direct attractive force of the city extended more widely, just as the industrial north began to lose some of its demographic magnetism. On the whole Ravenstein's model of population movement best fits Lanca-shire, the West Riding, the West Midlands and London, growing concentrations of population set in areas of fairly dense rural population. Other developing districts were not in this position, South Wales, Northumbria and Scotland for example, which as coalfields generated much of their own increase while as rapidly growing industrial communities in not very densely populated areas they attracted some migrants from afar.

South Wales provides an interesting example, in some respects exceptional, of the migrational component in nineteenth-century population growth. Glamorgan's population grew from 70,879 in 1801 to 231,849 in 1851 (still a lower density than rural Somerset) and more than a million by 1911. The initial force for growth was not coal but the iron on the northern margins of the coalfield. In 1851 Merthyr Tydfil, the county's largest town, had 40 per cent of its population natives of four nearby rural counties, Pembroke, Cardigan, Carmarthen and Brecon. Coalfield expansion, beginning in the east and spreading westwards, and the creation of the coal ports, called forth population increase beyond the possibility of supply from adjacent Welsh counties. Their contribution dropped from 70 per cent of all in-migration in 1861-71 to 40 per cent in 1871-81 as the total inflow rapidly increased. Population movement was no irrational rush to streets paved with gold however; it was sensitive to the state of the coal trade in terms of both numbers and distance — the slump of the 1890s reduced distant in-migration most conspicuously. Nevertheless by 1900 non-Welsh migrants outnumbered natives not only on the coast, as had long been the case, but in the mining interior, the traditional stronghold of the Welsh migrant with a more limited range of skills to sell. The overall pattern thus comprises a long-term trend — more non-Welsh immigrants, a degree of locational choice relating to migrant origins, and a sensitivity to the local economy manifest in the variable level of in-migration from distant parts.

RURAL DEPOPULATION

The converse of urban growth was evidently primarily a matter of out-migration although by the end of the century this had so affected the structure of some rural populations that they were failing to replace losses through death. The implications of rural depopulation were the subject of considerable contemporary discussion (almost as much in Britain as in France, if somewhat less emotionally). It was not a question of absolute and prolonged decline over wide areas but of continuing and widespread relative decline, absolute loss in some counties from mid-century and in some locations from rather earlier, and of the apparent age- and ability-selective character of rural out-migration and thus of its impact on rural social life and the rural economy. As used at this period the term 'rural depopulation' was less a precise statement than a vague complaint of real and imaginary ills. Moreover the geographical basis of rural out-migration lacked the apparent logic of coalfield-based industrial growth; it was a widespread phenomenon showing little correlation, spatial or temporal, with the century's several agricultural crises (save at a very local level and perhaps more widely at the margins of cultivation in the years immediately after 1815). Pull was proving more effective than push, witness the continuance of overpopulation and congestion in remote parts of the highland zone. How far the railways played a part is uncertain. Their influence is unlikely to have been great at the local level, but it was probably indispensable for long-distance movements. Canon Girdlestone[5] could scarcely have moved 600 farm labourers from Devon to the north in the 1860s without its aid. The role of a degree of breakdown in rural isolation towards the end of the century is equally uncertain — whether perhaps it became possible to live in the country and work in the town, likewise the converse.

EMIGRATION AND IMMIGRATION

Movement overseas from Britain has as long a history as internal migration and its characteristic nineteenth-century features are massive increase, widespread interest and improved document-ation. Whereas rural depopulation smacked of decadence, emigration might, at least from mid-century, be seen as a sign of fashionable virtues; self-help, initiative, enterprise and imperial vigour.

Emigration was a highly selective operation. Whether to go? Where to go? These questions had to be answered on the basis of even scantier information and understanding than that possessed by the internal migrant. In the severest crises these issues were unimportant, as to the Irish peasant in 1846. In general push factors were strongest early in the century and became weaker as it progressed; even so economic depression in the 1880s was one reason for a return of emigration to its highest level since the 1850s. As the century progressed it became easier to assess the opportunities presented by North America and the Antipodes and there were more organised schemes — no guarantee of success — and more official involvement. But such emigration booms as the gold rushes of the years after 1849 contained irrational as well as rational elements.

The greater part of the New World was farmland, at least potentially, and cheap land by Old World standards; it thus exercised a strong appeal to farmers and farm workers. But there was always a place for the skilled craftsman, especially as New World industrial economics developed, and for the young unmarried woman of any occupation or none. The cost of emigration, even to the U.S.A., was a barrier insurmountable to the very poor but not so considerable as to prevent many illiterate, unskilled and near destitute families heading overseas. At the other extreme some of the first Canterbury colonists, university graduates in many cases, watched their flocks by day and read the Latin and Greek classics by night.[6] There is some evidence that the stepwise migration process operated internationally, that the British conurbations as much as or more than the British countryside provided the stream of migrants. Many goldminers of the 1860s had a long migrant history, first to California, thence to Victoria and thence to New Zealand, and this kind of movement was not restricted to such peculiar occupations as the quest for gold.

The likeliest origin of the nineteenth-century emigrant Briton was then the highland zone, urban or rural, and an occupation undergoing crisis or change. On grounds of access, cheapness and size he was more likely to go to the U.S.A. than to the colonies.

But Britain was a land of immigrants as well as of emigrants. The Irish had come to Britain in small numbers as permanent settlers or seasonal workers before the catastrophe of 1846, after which date they became at first a flood, then a steady stream. The main ports of entry, Liverpool and Glasgow, acquired distinctive and persistent Irish enclaves; the former even returned an Irish Nationalist M.P. for its Scotland division between 1885 and 1929. In 1851 13 per cent of the population of Manchester and nine per cent of the population of Bradford was Irish — by 1871 nine per cent and six per cent respectively. The Irish were settling into the role of a minority group concentrated in the worst houses and jobs, practising a religion to which there was still a great deal of hostility, but they were a vital part of the community economically as well as demographically. By the end of the century other immigrant communities had established themselves — refugee Jews in London (in 1901 14 per cent of the population of Stepney was Russian- or Polish-born) and a cosmopolitan dockland community in Cardiff, where in 1901 three per cent of the population had been born outside the United Kingdom. The immigrant and the immigrant community belong to nineteenth- as well as to twentieth-century Britain.

PATTERNS OF SETTLEMENT

More people in new places created new patterns of settlement, of urban settlement in particular; they made new, often frightful, environments and new demands on resources. It was not however merely a matter of weight of numbers and blind economic forces. Deliberate attempts to improve the residential environment emanated from new knowledge and increased wealth, new architectural styles, new social attitudes — did not Prince Albert turn his hand to designing model cottages?[7] — new laws and new institutions. These same forces had unforeseen, and even unwelcome, effects on the geography of settlement; the back-to-back slums of the industrial north used the same materials as the most attractive country cottage, and in the broad sense were created within the same socio-economic environment. To look at the houses the Victorians and their immediate forbears built is at once to register a caveat against over-broad generalisation.

CENTRAL PLACES

Economic growth and a transport revolution generated changes in the system of central places — the. hierarchy of city, town, village, hamlet, farm and cottage — which have only begun to be explored. Many old towns ceased to function as central places to some degree, their markets dwindled, their range of shops and services diminished. On the other hand new towns of considerable importance in the national or even the worldwide economy were often central places for only a limited area and in a limited sense, not least because they were so close together.

The spacing of central places early in the nineteenth century varied from one part of the country to another, a consequence of differences of relief, resources, wealth, and historical accident. In East Anglia for example, rich but primarily rural and agricultural, Dickinson has shown that market towns were as little as eight miles apart in the wealthiest areas; he also showed that some of them were declining, as roads improved and rural industry decayed, even before the railways were built. Better communications threatened as many or more central places as they benefited. The railway, or more often its absence, was the *coup de grâce* of many small market towns throughout Britain, although Peake's suggestion[8] of as many as half the total by 1850 is surely an exaggeration. The problem of such towns was not that they became less accessible but that those favoured by the railway — in a few cases created by it, as was Craven Arms — became more accessible. It was the accessible centre which was attractive, both to the local customer and, to a greater extent, to buyer and seller from distant parts, such as the commercial traveller and the cattle dealer. A number of what might be regarded as ephemeral central places were also killed by the railways: the old seasonal livestock fairs, Weyhill and Stenhousemuir for example, dwindled and died as weekly markets in more accessible centres grew and flourished; perhaps some of the rotten boroughs which disappeared in 1832 might almost be regarded as ephemeral central places! By the end of the century the bicycle — and soon the car and bus — appeared as further agents of change, again favouring some larger and more central places over their smaller and peripheral rivals. However it might also be argued that with agricultural depression and rapidly rising living standards late in the century the agricultural market role of many country towns diminished and their importance as shopping and service centres increased, taking away some significance from the railways. Finally, in a number of cases industrial growth, in town or hinterland or both, provided a boost to established central place functions, as happened to many old market towns in South Wales as coalmining developed. The possible implications of the theme are immense and they still await the scrutiny of the geographer.

The new industrial towns were often traditional central places in only a limited sense, for to many of them their local setting was less important than worldwide markets, and their own population was far greater than that of the surrounding area for which they were a service centre. In this latter role retail trade was often well developed however, witness the continuing importance of street or covered markets in many northern industrial towns. Only a few such towns could fulfil traditional central place functions — a market for farmers, a seat for local or regional government. Mining communities and holiday resorts were similarly placed; superimposed upon an older system they served but a limited territory and that primarily for shopping or recreation; their *raison d'être* lay outside the old established system. A few settlements such as Brighton grew so large as to acquire a wider central place role and conversely a large number of specialised settlements shrank, disappeared or changed their character during the century — metalliferous mining communities in the Pennines and many of the lesser ports.

The smaller rural settlements — villages, townships or hamlets — likewise changed. A few grew into market or factory towns or holiday resorts, rather more lost some of their functional centrality, and reputedly their vitality, particularly in the latter half of the century. Early in the century the parish or township, the small rural community, still enjoyed a powerful political central place role. As the basic unit of local government it provided poor relief for those who had a 'settlement' there, and maintained the lesser roads. This was not an efficient system of local government and during the century these powers and rights passed to larger units, such as the Poor Law Unions of 1834. On the other hand population increase, higher real wages (especially for farm workers from mid-century) and perhaps changing taste and custom provided an increased range of shops in many villages. There were also more village schools and post offices, commonly nineteenth-century creations to serve new needs and a larger population. By the end of the century there are signs of some reversal of this situation, a consequence of rural depopulation and increased mobility. The pendulum was swinging back towards greater dependence on the urban central place and the individual's own resources than on village services.

The Cerne Abbas district (a Dorset Poor Law Union of twenty parishes) provides an example of the complexities of this situation in the latter half of the century. The population fell·from almost 8,000 in 1851 to little more than 5,000 in 1901, but the provision of retail services slightly improved from one shop to 34 inhabitants to one to 30; many more schools and post offices appeared. The larger villages providing the widest range of services lost not only proportionately more people but also more services; the smaller villages fared better in this respect, perhaps because the advent of school and post office removed a reason for their inhabitants to visit a larger centre. Cerne Abbas itself, a small town not served by the railway, fared very badly. Of the 57 fewer tradesmen in the area in 1901 than 1851, 46 had disappeared from Cerne Abbas and nine from Sydling St Nicholas, another large village. Political and administrative centrality was however retained, since the workhouse, Petty Sessional Court and even a new Rural District Council remained in Cerne Abbas, a situation which did not survive for very long. Commercial functions were lost more readily than administrative – personal decisions are more speedily taken than political. In sum, the changes which occurred reduced large villages and a small town to lower positions in the hierarchy, probably in part because of the remoteness from the railway, rather than making for an overall deterioration in service provision.

The changing commercial central place system contained a large element of logic and order. This was not the case in matters of politics and administration above the decreasingly important parish level. Rather there developed 'a curiously confusing reticulation of mutually intrusive and intersecting jurisdictions' – 'a chaos as regards authorities, a chaos as regards rates, and a worse chaos than all as regards areas'.[10] Until late in the century an *ad hoc* tradition remained stronger than either that of rationalisation or consolidation. Thus within the area of

West Derby (Poor Law) Union (Lancashire) in 1881 lay all or part of ten local boards, one borough, one board of guardians, three burial boards, one school board and one highway board. In 1882 G. J. Goschen M.P. noted, as he later recalled, that he received 87 separate rate demands on a property worth £1,100, the smallest eight for a total of two shillings and fourpence. Reorganisation late in the century (1894) defied the hierarchical logic of central place theory and practice by regarding urban areas as enclaves and separating their local government from that of the countryside. Only in one important instance, the relief of the poor, was a more rational system adopted. This was one of the major concerns of nineteenth-century local government, the one the ordinary citizen was most likely to experience and which, to judge from grandparental reminiscence, was most feared. The Unions of parishes created for this purpose in 1834 were deliberately set up as a central place system - 'the most convenient limit of unions which we have found has been that of a circle, taking a market town as centre and comprehending those surrounding parishes whose inhabitants are accustomed to resort to the same market'[11] − for convenience of management. As such systems focused on the workhouse in the central place[12] the Unions cut across traditional boundaries of hundreds and even counties. Later the unions became the basis of rural districts but, as has been noted, they were decapitated in the process. The fact that they crossed county lines also influenced later changes in county boundaries; nevertheless they remain the great exception to a tradition of local government poorly correlated with central place systems.

NEW FORMS OF SETTLEMENT

The transition from a rural agricultural society to an urban industrial economy not only reorganised the central place system but also created new kinds of settlement. In fact most were not really new. The isolated farmsteads of enclosure and reclamation, mining and fishing villages, decaying market towns and holiday resorts, were certainly more numerous than ever before and with the coming of the railway their forms and details changed. But it is easy to trace their ancestry and recognise their forbears. Three much more novel, if not completely new, forms of settlement are the factory community, the suburb, and the conurbation. The first was produced by rapid economic and demographic growth in the absence of cheap and efficient means of transport; the second by the same forces in a setting of relative affluence, a shorter working day, and the horse-bus, tram, or railway. The two converge to produce the third, albeit to a varying degree. London was pre-eminently the product of suburban growth, the northern conurbations of the coalescence of mill communities, suburbs, and even pit villages. By the end of the century even country towns, except the most moribund, were experiencing suburban growth. 'Newtown' is a commonplace of Britain's nineteenth-century urban growth from Milborne Port to Manchester.

As yet the mill, mine or factory community lacks a generic name to match suburb or conurbation. It is not quite exclusively a nineteenth-century phenomenon; its burgeoning begins late in the eighteenth century and its origins even earlier, but only during the nineteenth century did it become widespread. A combination of circumstances created such places. Much early nineteenth-century industrial growth took place beside fast-flowing streams or, and to an increasing extent, on the coalfields; there were only canals and carthorses to move coal to consumers, and no means, other than walking, of moving worker to workplace and home again on a daily basis. Industrial Britain owes much of its character to this precocious industrialisation, prior to the building of the railways. Many of the areas affected were thinly peopled because they were agriculturally unattractive. Their labour force had to be imported, at least initially, and housed as close to their workplace and as cheaply as possible. Thus terraces and blocks were built alongside factories and mines in a hitherto rural setting. They were a new kind of community, imposed upon but not integrated into the rural scene, narrow in their occupational structure, limited in the range of services they provided. At worst they were unplanned, ungoverned, undrained and unorganised, monotonous and compact streets of overcrowded and jerry-built houses (plate 4). They were, like the factories they served, expected to provide a profit. Yet in a minority of cases they were model environments, New Lanark or Saltaire for example. In both instances they outlived the circumstances of their creation: the worst became slums, already being demolished by the second half of the century, and the surviving best are as much monuments worthy of preservation as Stonehenge or Salisbury Cathedral.

The suburb, and its close cousin the satellite or dormitory community, are an inherently more varied phenomenon than the factory town, and a very much older one. They share with these industrial settlements a nineteenth-century transformation, but one embracing a much wider range of social classes. The wealthy Evangelicals of the Clapham Sect[13] commuted from a fashionable suburb whereas the continuous line of houses along the Manchester-Oldham road by 1848 represents a less attractive form. Conversely London had a hollow core, a dead heart, by 1800, and such major cities as Glasgow and Birmingham by mid-century. As villages became accessible by horse-bus, tram or even railway, their populations were increased by those who were thus able to leave the city while continuing to work there; such villages often moved down the social scale, as Islington did for example. At the same time new houses were built along or close to the roads linking the urban core to these suburban nuclei, old and new, and then beyond them there was ribbon development as it is commonly called. Much the same might happen along a railway, particularly if its policy was to encourage commuter traffic, an example of which was the Great Eastern in north-east London. The final stage, before redevelopment, was the infilling of the interstices of open space between ribbon and nuclear development. Unforeseen access problems and the use of such space for activities as environmentally destructive as brickmaking might make this a protracted process; surprisingly large areas of undeveloped, even derelict, land thus survive in many suburbs.

The process and product of suburban growth can be related to several factors, the existing template of settlement and communications, changing means (and costs) of transport and the attitude of those providing it, the attitudes and abilities of landowners, local authorities, financial institutions and builders, none of them homogenous groups. The suburb also reflected changes in taste and fashion and in its own social standing – as the century progresses there is an increasing resemblance between working class suburb and factory community in outward appearance. By and large the historical geography of the suburb remains unexplored, Dyos's work on Camberwell being an obvious exception. The time is ripe for such a shift in emphasis, as appears to be beginning, in the study of the urban past.

The conurbation emerges as the combination and climax of urban growth, the fusion of parts into a whole. Geddes coined the word only in 1915 to describe 'these city-regions, these town aggregates'[14] (and as much in terms of becoming as of being) still in a formative stage in most cases. Ought the term to be used only of a continuously built-up area, or more loosely? Should it be conceived in terms of space, function, or population? Britain's conurbations were in fact quite small in 1900 — Manchester for example was but tenuously linked to Eccles, Chorlton and Didsbury. But the nineteenth century had witnessed striking population increase and the West Yorkshire conurbation was, in this sense, already half its present size by 1851; central Clydeside had a million and a half people by 1901. London might by any criteria be regarded as a conurbation by 1801 and other cities passed into this category during the century, creating and swallowing suburbs, embracing a diversity of economic and social activities, establishing an internal central place heirarchy for such matters as shopping. Their system of local government rarely kept up with their growth, their spatial spread in particular. London soon outgrew such recognitions of its special position as the Metropolitan Police of 1829 and the London County Council of 1888. However the inadequacies of local government did not prevent ambitious schemes of central redevelopment, sometimes deliberately associated with the clearance of overcrowded and insanitary districts. Edinburgh provided a magnificent model, emulated by Newcastle upon Tyne and in some degree by London, but too rarely matched in the suburbs and too often destroyed in the 1960s and 1970s.

A NEW FABRIC OF SETTLEMENT

New factories, new churches, and above all new houses had to be built to meet the economic, spiritual, and domestic needs of a growing population. The now inner, often decaying, suburbs of Bristol and Tyneside for example, reflect this need and the way it was met; new cottages, new farm buildings in the countryside were less numerous, but they too reflect the socio-economic circumstances in which they were created. For most of the century the concept of private property and its rights was better developed — and defended — than that of public interest and so the need for housing was generally interpreted in terms of commercial enterprise and private profit. Housing was expected to pay, generally to pay well; even philanthropic housing trusts more often than not operated as dividend- or interest-paying institutions. Housing also had to be paid for and low incomes were probably the most important among many constraints upon quality, but even the middle class who could afford to pay endured defective drains and shoddy masonry (plate 5).

Nineteenth-century builders, developers and speculators operated in a legislative framework minimal by the standards of the 1970s but certainly not non-existent. There occurred a transition from minimum and ineffective control through localised and permissive laws until considerable quality control (but rarely locational control, the quintessence of modern planning) was achieved in the last quarter of the century. Environmental quality was seen as an apt area for legislation earliest in the century with respect to workplace, the more conspicuously dangerous in particular; then, after a period of activity on a voluntary basis, with respect to the setting of the residence or workplace in matters such as water supply, drainage and refuse collection (not of open space provision however) likely to offend or infect the middle class passer-by; and last of all with respect to the structure of the house itself. 'An Englishman's home is his castle'! A mass of often unworkable legislation was created. Urban Improvement Commissioners, concerned with the watch (a rudimentary police) paving and lighting, had existed since the eighteenth century and provided a tradition to build upon. Much nineteenth-century legislation was early and enlightened: Manchester controlled street and court width from 1830, prohibited cellar dwellings from 1853, insisted on water closets from 1881 and damp courses from 1890. But permissive legislation depended upon the inherently changeable attitude of the local authority, thus Manchester also appointed no Medical Officer of Health until 1868 and then limited his activities, a generation after more progressive towns had acted.[15] Even the greatest acts of environmental legislation were largely permissive, the Public Health Act of 1848, Torrens's and Cross's Housing Acts of 1868 and 1875 respectively, the Public Health Act of 1875. Back-to-back housing was forbidden to the speculative builder only in 1925. Implementation depended on the energy and policy of the local authority, the aim being to set standards for the future rather than to remedy the mistakes of the past. Nevertheless housing was marked down as an appropriate area for government intervention and basic principles, such as the duty of the owner to keep the house in good repair, were established. This latter problem was as acute a hundred years ago as it is now for overcrowded, jerry-built nineteenth-century houses were very prone to the dilapidation and disrepair of even the limited amenities provided.

Pre-eminent among nineteenth-century building materials was brick, particularly after the extension of the canal and railway networks had made it cheaply available almost everywhere. Cheapness was an important matter not only in terms of the working man's ability to pay to be housed but also of the economy's ability to support the huge cost of housing a larger population, even in an indifferent fashion. Thus cheap bricks ousted not only stone but a rich variety of more costly local bricks, in Middlesex for example. Similarly, if less generally, Welsh slate became the commonest roofing material. Stone and other expensive or exotic materials were kept for the most part for prestige buildings, in remote areas, or near to the source of supply. By 1900 brick was triumphant even in some of the most substantially stone-built towns such as Sherborne, where for much of the century it had been no more than a rare intruder. The industrialisation of brick making followed upon rather than created this wider market; machinery for brick manufacture was perfected only in mid-century, the great brickworks like Fletton only in the last decades. Timber had for the most part to be imported and thus, for example, the fortunes of the timber trade at Poole, primarily with Baltic ports, relate closely to the growth of Bournemouth and its suburbs. The technology and organisation of the building industry, house building in particular, lagged even further behind. The new factories of the 1890s might be striking and sophisticated technological monuments, but the house builder still used large quantities of cheap and casual labour to place brick upon brick, even if those bricks might now comprise a damp course and enclose a water closet.

Brick could create a Bryanston or a Bedford Park, but for the most part it was used for small and simple houses meeting, sometimes ingeniously, existing legal requirements. A handful of basic designs covered thousands of acres with some adjustment to the special problems of hilly sites and some minor variation of fashion or ornament. Among widespread early nineteenth-century forms the 'not through' (plate 6) and the 'back-to-back' (figure 9) with common yard, pump, and earth closets were commonplace, as were irregular courtyard arrangements around such amenities. Vestiges of eighteenth-century classicism (plate 7) may appear in their fronts, the veneer of which often hid an appalling situation of disrepair, dirt, darkness and decay. The 'tunnel backs' built later in the century

Figure 9. 'Back-to-back' housing as built in Nottingham between c. 1784 and 1830. Domestic industry was the norm in this city at this date (see Chapter 5), hence the workroom; compare also plate 4. It should also be remembered that it was not uncommon for more than one family to occupy a house. (Redrawn from Chapman, S.D., (ed.), *The History of Working-class Housing : a symposium*, Newton Abbot, 1971, figure 4.1.)

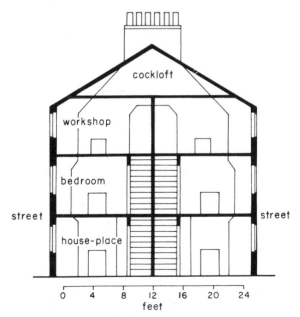

solved the problem of an increasing degree of legislative control; they survive as a common setting for the arrival by train at any major railway station. The form solved the problem not as one devised by the law, nor as a pleasant urban environment, but as the builder's successful attempt to maximise density and minimise cost within the terms of new legislation. The monotony of such order and fashion is however an improvement on the monotony of chaos and squalor, and by the era of the 'tunnel back'[16] a good water supply and a regular refuse collection were adding an element of safety and decency to the urban scene. Local forms — the flat house of Tyneside, the Scottish bungalow or tenement — were created and persisted. By 1900 a few communities designed for working class families were setting standards not always matched in new housing a lifetime later, Bournville and Port Sunlight for example.

Nineteenth-century problems and failures in the area of building in general and housing in particular are now less often derided than even a generation ago.[17] Not only is Victoriana again fashionable but a wealthy society unable adequately to house its citizens is less inclined to scoff at its poorer forbears who, according to their own standards and without crippling their economy, housed an extra 27 million people in the course of a century. They were housed, they lived with a strong prospect of material improvement within their lifetime. How did they earn their living?

NOTES

1 Clark, G.S.R. Kitson, *The Making of Victorian England*, London, 1962. p.64.

2 This unsatisfactory system was initiated by the 1844 Factory Act and lingered on until 1922, but numbers were very few after 1900.

3 Cairncross, A.K., *Home and foreign investment 1870-1913*, Cambridge, 1953, p.79.

4 MacDonald, D.F., *Scotland's shifting population 1770-1850*. Glasgow, 1937, p.87, quoting the *Statistical Accounts*, a detailed contemporary survey.

5 Vicar of Halberton, Devon, from 1862 to 1872, and earlier a curate and incumbent in Lancashire. There seems little

doubt that the contrast between conditions in the two areas roused him to action. He became a prominent member of a minority of 'radical' clergy, reviled by many landowners, farmers and fellow clergy.

6 The best known example, Samuel Butler, used a New Zealand setting for his Utopian novel *Erewhon*. He wrote of his experiences as a colonist in *A First Year In Canterbury Settlement*, 1863.

7 For the Great Exhibition of 1851, where it was awarded the Gold Medal in Class VII.

8. Peake, H.J.E., 'Geographical aspects of administative areas', *Geography*, Vol. 15, 1930, pp. 531-46.

9 For a description see the opening chapter of Thomas Hardy, *The Mayor of Casterbridge*.

10 Lipman, V.D., *Local Government Areas: 1834-1945*, Oxford, 1949, pp. 78 and 81, the latter quoting Goschen.

11 Quoted by Lipman, p. 44.

12 Since many workhouses survive as geriatric hospitals so, in a curious way, has their central place role. Our treatment of the elderly retains some nineteenth-century characteristics!

13 The best known was William Wilberforce, leader of the movement for the abolition of slavery.

14 Geddes, P., *Cities in Evolution*, London, 1915, p. 34.

15 Charles Kingsley's novels *Yeast*, *Alton Locke*, and *Two Years Ago* all relate to mid-century sanitary problems.

16 So called because they were built in terraces, access to the rear of the houses being by tunnels passing through the terrace.

17 A delightful satirical but by no means unsympathetic account of the forms of later nineteenth century urban growth is to be found in the later chapters of Osbert Lancaster's *Draynflete Revealed*.

FURTHER READING

1 POPULATION

Cairncross, A.K., 'Internal migration in Victorian England', *Manchester School*, vol. 17, 1949, pp. 67-87.

Carrier, N.H., and Jeffery, J.R., 'External migration: a study of the available statistics', *Studies on Medical and Population*

Subjects, vol. 6, London (General Register Office), 1953.

Darby, H.C., 'The movement of population to and from Cambridgeshire between 1851 and 1861', *Geographical Journal*, vol. 101, 1943, pp. 118-25.

Deane, P. and Cole, W.A., *British Economic Growth 1688-1959: Trends and Structures*, Cambridge 1967, ch. 3, 'Industrialisation and population change in the eighteenth and early nineteenth centuries'.

Law, C.M., 'The growth of urban population in England and Wales 1801-1911', *Institute of British Geographers: Transactions*, vol. 41, 1967, pp. 125-44.

Lawton, R., 'The population of Liverpool in the mid-nineteenth century', *Transactions of the Historical Society of Lancashire and Cheshire*, vol. 107, 1955, pp. 89-120.

Lawton, R., 'Population movements in the West Midlands 1841-61', *Geography*, vol. 43, pp. 164-77.

Lawton, R., 'Population changes in England and Wales in the later nineteenth century', *Institute of British Geographers: Transactions*, vol. 44, 1968, pp. 55-74.

Lawton, R., 'Rural depopulation in nineteenth century England', in Steel, R.W., and Lawton, R., *Liverpool Essays in Geography*, Liverpool, 1967, pp. 227-55.

MacDonald, D.F., *Scotland's shifting population 1770-1850*, Glasgow, 1937.

McKeown, T., and Record, R.G., 'Reasons for the decline of mortality in England and Wales during the nineteenth century', *Population Studies*, vol. 16, 1962-3, pp. 94-122.

McKeown, T., Brown, R.G., and Record, R.G., 'The modern rise of population in Europe', *Population Studies*, vol. 26, 1972-3, pp. 345-82.

Osborne, R.H., 'The movements of people in Scotland 1851-1951', *Scottish Studies*, vol. 2, 1958, pp. 1-46.

Ravenstein, E.G., 'The laws of migration', *Journal of the Royal Statistical Society*, vol. 48, 1885, pp. 167-235.

Redford, A., *Labour migration in England 1800-1850*, 2nd edition revised by Chaloner, W.H., Manchester, 1964.

Smith, C.T., 'The movement of population in England and Wales in 1851 and 1861', *Geographical Journal*, vol. 117, 1951, pp. 200-10.

Thomas, B., 'The migration of labour into the Glamorganshire coalfield 1861-1911', *Economica*, vol. 10, 1930, pp. 275-94.

Trueman, Sir A.E., 'Population changes in the eastern part of the South Wales coalfield', *Geographical Journal*, vol. 53, 1919, pp. 410-19.

Wallis, B.C., 'Nottinghamshire in the nineteenth century: geographical factors in the growth of the population', *Geographical Journal*, vol. 43, 1914, pp. 34-61.

Welton, T.A., 'On the distribution of the population in England and Wales . . . 1801-91', *Journal of the Royal Statistical Society*, vol. 63, 1900, pp. 527-89.

Wrigley, E.A., *Population and History*, London, 1969.

2   SETTLEMENT

Ashworth, W., *The Genesis of Modern Town Planning*, London, 1954.

Bowley, M., *Innovations in building materials*, London, 1960.

Carter, H., *The Towns of Wales*, Cardiff, 1965.

Carter, H., 'Urban grades in south-west Wales: an historical consideration', *Scottish Geographical Magazine*, vol. 71, 1955, pp. 43-58.

Dickinson, R.E., 'The distribution and functions of the smaller urban settlements of East Anglia', *Geography*, vol. 17, 1932, pp. 19-31.

Dyos, H.J., 'The slums of Victorian London', *Victorian Studies*, vol. 11, 1967-8, pp. 5-40.

Dyos, H.J., 'The speculative builders and developers of Victorian London', *Victorian Studies*, vol. 11 (supplement), 1967-8, pp. 641-90

Dyos, H.J., *Victorian suburb: a study of the growth of Camberwell*, London, 1961.

Frazer, W.M., *History of English public health 1834-1939*, London, 1950.

Gauldie, E., *Cruel Habitations: a history of working-class housing 1780-1918*, London, 1974.

Lipman, V.C., *Local Government Areas 1834-1945*, Oxford, 1949.

Newton, R., *Victorian Exeter*, Leicester, 1968.

Simon, E.D., and Inman, J., *The Rebuilding of Manchester*, London, 1935.

Smailes, A.E., 'The urban grid of England and Wales', *Institute of British Geographers: Transactions and Papers*, vol. 11, 1946, pp. 87-101.

Tarn, J.N., *Five per cent Philanthropy: An Account of Housing in Urban Areas between 1840 and 1914*, Cambridge, 1973.

3 Mines and Metals: The Geography of Basic Industry

The answer to the rhetorical question posed at the end of the preceding chapter lies in the phrase 'the workshop of the world'. A growing population was sustained and higher living standards were attained by selling raw materials, manufactured goods, and services to the world at large. The bases of this activity were Britain's enormous and accessible reserve of coal, and the technology which exploited it and which matched it to a substantial but less generous reserve of iron ore.

COAL AND STEAM

Among possible themes around which a historical geography of nineteenth-century Britain might be written, coal is pre-eminent. At the end of the century coalmining employed over a million people. Coal was the motive force of Britain and the economically developed world for ships, for railways, for machinery; it was a major export staple, a chemical raw material, a domestic fuel, and not least a locational force. It even begins to appear in the 1970s that present-day dependence on oil and gas may turn out to be no more than an interregnum in the age of coal. Coal was king: 'all the activity and industry of this kingdom is fast concentrating where there are coal pits'[1] wrote Arthur Young as early as 1791. Even by this date precocious industrial development had begun to lay down an industrial geography on the coalfields, half a century before a railway network capable of distributing so bulky a source of power was created.

Britain's coal output increased from about 11 million tons in

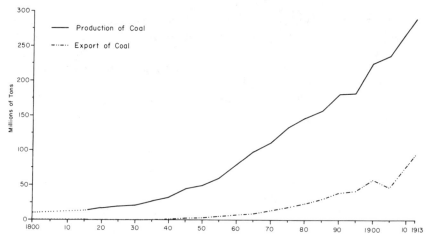

Figure 10. Britain's coal output and exports, 1800-1913. (Drawn from five-yearly date in Deane, P., and Cole, W.A. *British Economic Growth 1688-1959*, Cambridge, 1962, table 54.)

1800 to more than 225 million in 1900 (figure 10), a revolution in itself. An industry made up of small family-owned enterprises in the early nineteenth century, located on the exposed fields, employing no more than a few hundred men to dig a few hundred feet deep, had become in most areas an industry dominated by colliery companies employing several thousand men and sinking shafts as deep as 3,000 feet into 'concealed' coal fields. In the process mining had become safer, largely through legislative action — in the 1850s there were about 4.3 deaths per year for every thousand workers, by the 1900s only 1.4 per thousand.

The early nineteenth-century industry was still largely concerned with traditional domestic and industrial markets, Durham with London, South Wales with its iron-masters for example. Accessibility was of prime importance and until at least mid-century coastal coalfields maintained their long-standing advantage over those of the interior. Thus as late as 1847 the Rhonnda was described as 'the gem of South Wales . . . hardly surpassed throughout the Alpine North'.[2] Railways opened up such inland districts and 'brought a measure of unity to an industry which had hitherto been distinguished by its diversity'.[3] It was only a measure; numerous small workings for local markets survived in such areas as the Forest of Dean, and large regional combines, such as were characteristic of the development of the German coal industry after 1880, were rare. As coal is not a uniform commodity in its own characteristics or in those of its occurrence, mining or marketing, so methods of production, costs, wages and social conditions were as diverse in 1900 as in 1800. They were made more conspicuously so by the size and importance of the industry and the extent to which the government involved itself in its affairs.

Technical changes were unspectacular compared to those in the iron and steel industry or inland transport; coal remained a labour intensive, 'pick and shovel' industry. At the very end of the century a mere three per cent of Scottish coal was machine cut, and Scotland was a pioneering area in this activity.[4] Mechanisation, like other innovations, proceeded discontinuously and at different dates in different fields. Some technical advances are well known, such as the safety lamp and legislative insistence on at least two shafts from 1862.[5] Most are not; in South Wales for example the spread of the longwall method of working in the 1860s, the use of compressed air from about 1865, and improved ventilation by means of fans in the third quarter of the century. Nationwide such advances sustained productivity increase in the face of the inevitable problems of deeper pits, longer underground hauls, and the exhaustion of the thickest and most accessible seams, so that an average output of 220 tons per man per year in 1851 reached 326 tons by the early eighties. Thereafter productivity slowly fell back, not that mining became a technological laggard by comparison with overseas producers — as yet scarcely competitors — the commonplace criticism of late Victorian industry. The problems were organisational and historical, related to such issues as limited finance and bad working conditions. 'The weakness of the early twentieth century coal industry was not that it was under-capitalised . . . but that its assets were too thinly and unevenly spread.'[6] Some degree of weakness and vulnerability is inherent in an old-established extractive industry; some was related to the attitudes of masters and men. Whatever the dimensions of these problems they were, until the 1920s, more often than not concealed by buoyant demand.

The demand for coal in the early nineteenth century contained two components, the domestic and the industrial. Householders needed coal for heating and for cooking; industrialists used coal to raise steam, to boil and evaporate liquids (brine for example) and as a chemical raw material, notably in the manufacture of iron. In every case the coastal, canal-side, or coalfield consumer was in a favoured position — elsewhere coal was because of its bulk a costly raw material, often a luxury. The areas served by the English coalfields appear on a map prepared for the Royal Commission of 1830 (figure 11); the pre-eminence of the north-east coast with its dominance of the London market is evident. There were other coastal fields, among them Fifeshire and Cumberland, and inland fields serving local markets.

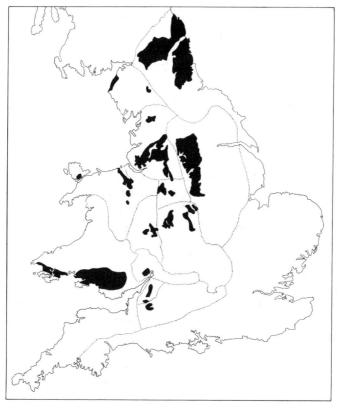

Figure 11. Britain's coalfields and their markets in 1830. (Redrawn from Clapham, J.B., *An Economic History of Modern Britain*, Volume 1 ('The early railway age'), Cambridge, 1926, facing p.236, in turn based on *Report of the Select Committee on the Coal Trade*, 1830.)

Coal and iron were associated not only technologically but also geologically, since black-band iron ores occur in the coal measures. By the early nineteenth century this association had a long enough history in Coalbrookdale to drive the iron industry eastward into an area requiring deeper collieries. Shropshire may be regarded as the heartland of this coal-iron relationship, but it was also strong elsewhere. The Ayrshire and Clackmannanshire coalfield served the Devon ironworks (near Clackmannan burgh), the iron industry placed Lanark first among Scottish coalfields, and ironmasters opened up the northern part of the South Wales coalfields in the early nineteenth century. West coast coalfields, Ayrshire for example, could also look to coalless Ireland as a market. The market was, however, changing; industrial demand was more and more for steam, for by the 1830s cotton was essentially a steam industry. In the iron trade Nielsen's hot-blast process of 1828 reduced coal requirements by about two-thirds; in fact as iron production was growing and the process was not adopted instantaneously there was no absolute diminution in the industry's demand for coal, but the tight locational bond of coal to iron had for the first time been loosened.

The great nineteenth-century turning point for the coal industry is however the 1840s. The great expansion of the railway network provided a new and enormous market for steam coal while it facilitated both mining in and the supply of coal to interior Britain. The continuing growth of the industrial economy, driven by steam, likewise extended the market and such enterprises as Bute Dock (Cardiff, 1839) opened up overseas trade. Between 1830 and 1860 output increased almost fourfold to reach 80 million tons, and by the latter date Britain's share of world production was three-fifths. This was the very foundation of Britain's mid-century growth and pre-eminence, so much so as to lead the older Jevons, pessimistic as to the extent of coal reserves, to a 'gloomy forecast: 'we have to make the choice between brief greatness and longer continued mediocrity'.[7] The north-east coast, the old established producer of high grade steam coal, gradually lost pre-eminence to South Wales, at first to the more accessible Aberdare valleys, later to the Rhonnda. Former ironmasters became primarily mineowners in these areas, their well-established pits having an initial advantage over new, remote, high-wage ventures. By the 1860s the steamship had become an important coal consumer although this market, like overseas exports, reached its apogee only late in the century. The steamer was not, unlike the train, an almost instantaneous success. Mid-century was also the heyday of the black-band iron industry, coal-field based and the *raison d'être* of many collieries in the secondary fields, such as in Scotland. These were the depressed areas of 1920s in the making, where iron works and mines were established which could not carry on seventy years later when coal and iron resources were almost exhausted and prices low. Already by mid-century deeper pits and migration to the concealed field were becoming widely necessary, a development begun in Shropshire fifty years or so earlier, extended to the north east in the 1820s and to the East Midlands in the 1850s. In this expansion the London market played a large part, witness the extensive coal yards to the north of London's northern railway termini. Some secondary fields developed almost wholly for this market at this date, the Leicestershire-South Derbyshire coalfield for example.

The second turning point occurs some time in the 1870s. Productivity per man reached its peak about 1880, thereafter to fall as cheap labour was used as an alternative to machinery. The labour force in fact grew faster than the population, but a continuous influx of new labour into the mines necessarily lowered output per man per hour and thus raised coal prices (mining was by no means an unskilled industry). To some extent this trend was countered by the lessened seasonality of the coal trade as household markets became proportionately less important. The late nineteenth-century coal industry was then a business of mass labour, of limited companies (replacing the older partnerships), and of the pre-eminence of steam coal for shipping and export. This latter situation particularly favoured South Wales. Coal had become a producer good, subject at times to insatiable demand but also vulnerable to trade recession and even to foreign competition. Thus growth was more erratic and less rapid than in mid-century, doubling between 1870 and 1900 where it had trebled in the preceding thirty years. Industrial strife was also important in this context.

By 1900 exports, almost 50 million tons a year, accounted for one quarter of total output (figures 12 and 13). They were made up largely of steam coal from two fields: South Wales sent

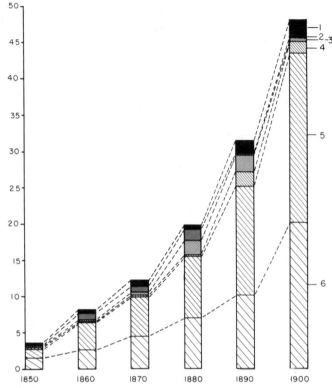

Figure 12. Britain's export trade in coal 1850-1900, in millions of tons, by destination: 1, South America and Pacific ports of U.S.A., (Colombia and Venezuela excepted); 2, North and Central America, Colombia and Venezuela; 3, East Africa, Asia and Australasia; 4, West and South Africa; 5, France and the Mediterranean; 6, Baltic ports, Germany and the Low Countries. (Drawn from Thomas, D.A., 'The growth and direction of our foreign trade in coal during the last half century', *Journal of the Royal Statistical Society*, Vol. 66, 1903, appendix C, p.508.)

two-fifths of its output overseas through an elaborate system of railways and their docks created during the century and the north-east coast exported one-third of its production via older established channels. Lower freights facilitated export — the rate to Buenos Aires was 35s 6d per ton in 1863, 16s in 1900, the Argentine railways being an important market. More efficient steamers and a general deflation combined to provide the world with cheap coal, and by 1900 85 per cent of this

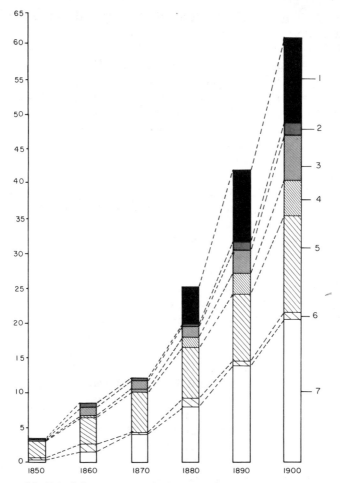

Figure 13. Britain's export trade in coal 1850-1900, in millions of tons, by origin: 1, bunkers in foreign trade (no data for 1850-70); 2, West Scotland; 3, East Scotland; 4, Humber and East Coast ports south of Tees; 5, Durham, Northumberland, and Teesside; 6, North-west England; 7, Bristol Channel. (Drawn from same source as figure 12, p.509.)

international trade was British. Europe, the Mediterranean and South America were markets almost completely dominated by Britain, but in more distant areas, the Pacific for example, only passenger liner operators could stand the cost of shipping best Welsh steam coal in the face of local competition. 'The coal that saved Calliope'[8] came from the Buller rather than the Rhonnda. Coal export was not however merely a matter of direct earnings, since an outward coal cargo ensured that British vessels need rarely travel in ballast, enabling shipowners to offer competitive rates. As early as 1865 this was an important advantage.

Coal was the basis of late nineteenth-century British maritime supremacy, as export cargo as much as motive power. A more mundane parallel is the fact that coal royalties enabled many landowners to survive the agricultural crisis of this same period, in the West Riding for example. There remained a home market consuming more than 150 million tons a year — railways, houses, factories, gas and now electricity undertakings, and iron and steel works. These last now used one-eighth of total output where once they had used one-third. In general coal was used more effectively late in the century; the domestic hearth still pushed much of its heat — to say nothing of its smoke — up the chimney, but possibly as little as one-tenth of the coal required to raise one horse power in 1800 was needed for the same purpose in 1900. Flourishing markets for an extractive industry called for new sources of supply; new areas of production were developed, such as the Ashington district in Northumberland, while the industry in general migrated from old exposed fields to new concealed ones. The pits which had given so much impetus to Manchester and Bradford began to close, and coal itself lost a great deal of its locational power.

A 20-fold increase in output since 1800 and a five-fold increase in labour force since 1841 transformed the landscape of the coalfields. The deep mines of the latter part of the century were less directly destructive than their shallow predecessors, closely spaced and prone to subsidence. On the other hand they required miles of rail and tramway, created huge waste-tips, and since they required a larger labour force they created larger communities. New miners, locally born or immigrant, required new houses, usually cheek by jowl with the pit. The miners' row became as distinctive a part of the landscape of mining as the colliery winding gear. A number of circumstances combined to favour a settlement pattern at best drab and monotonous, at worst dreadful, although the rural setting of many such communities provided a redeeming feature. Much coalmining took place in a harsh physical environment, in Wales for example, where difficult sites for

house building favoured high densities; rapid growth of population where the industry grew rapidly led to overcrowding.
Housing the miner was expected to be profitable — and thus
cheap — an attitude favoured by the inherent risk that a new
mining venture would fail and be abandoned. Thus temporary
wooden barracks were sometimes built and acquired a particularly bad reputation. Some idea of the appalling conditions in
which the miner might be expected to live is provided by an
Ayrshire County Council Housing Committee resolution of
June 1914 — 'privies should have doors and seats'.[9] The mining
village was moreover often isolated, commonly made up solely
of workers at one pit, and thus economically and socially
vulnerable. These were veritable new towns — Tonypandy and
Cowdenbeath — but without the carefully planned housing and
social provision of their mid-twentieth-century counterparts.

The colliery owner might support churches and schools, but
the chapels and clubs of Durham, the West Riding and South
Wales owe much more to the miner. Regional social differences
related however not only to living and working conditions, the
latter enshrined in official wage differentials, but to cultural
antecedents. The Welsh valleys lost their language but retained
their music and their religious non-conformity; collections
among the mining communities sustained the infant Aberyst-
wyth University College. The cultural antecedents of the leek
clubs of Durham and Northumberland are obscure, but they
serve to emphasise the existence of distinct coalfield cultural
communities. The younger Jevons, writing in 1915, claimed
that in general the older coalfields provided the highest quality
of life, in part because the skill of the miner and the division of
labour there reached the highest level, in Scotland for example.
Newer coalfields, such as the East Midlands, provided a coarser
and cruder life style. In any event by 1900 the miner was
beginning to be able to live at a distance from his work; as well
as miners' rows there were extensive services of workmens'
trains, some in the Welsh valleys. The collier had become a
commuter.

But let D.H. Lawrence have the last word on the colliery
community and landscape:

> The string of coal-mines of B.W. & Co. had been opened
> some sixty years before I was born, and Eastwood had come
> into being as a consequence. It must have been a tiny village

at the beginning of the nineteenth century, a small place of
cottages and fragmentary rows of little four-roomed miners'
dwellings, the homes of the colliers of the eighteenth
century, who worked in the bits of mines, foot-hill mines
with an opening in the hillside into which the miners walked,
or windlass mines, where the men were wound up one at a
time, in a bucket, by a donkey. The windlass mines were still
working when my father was a boy — and the shafts of some
were still there, when I was a boy.

But somewhere about 1820 the company must have sunk
the first big shaft — not very deep — and installed the first
machinery of the real industrial colliery . . . My grandfather
settled in an old cottage down in a quarrybed, by the brook
at Old Brinsley, near the pit. A mile away, up at Eastwood,
the company built the first miners' dwellings — it must be
nearly a hundred years ago. Now Eastwood occupies a lovely
position on a hilltop, with the steep slope towards Derbyshire
and the long slope towards Nottingham. They put up a new
church, which stands fine and commanding, even if it has no
real form, looking across the awful Erewash Valley at the
church of Heanor, similarly commanding, away on a hill
beyond. What opportunities, what opportunities! These
mining villages might have been like the lovely hill-towns of
Italy, shapely and fascinating. And what happened?

Most of the little rows of dwellings of the old-style miners
were pulled down, and dull little shops began to rise along
the Nottingham Road, while on the down-slope of the north
side the company erected what is still known as the New
Buildings, or the Square. These New Buildings consist of two
great hollow squares of dwellings planked down on the rough
slope of the hill, little four-room houses with the 'front'
looking outward into the grim, blank street, and the 'back',
with a tiny square brick yard, a low wall, and a w.c. and
ash-pit, looking into the desert of the square, hard, uneven,
jolting black earth tilting rather steeply down, with these
little back yards all round, and openings at the corners. The
squares were quite big, and absolutely desert save for the
posts for clothes lines, and people passing, children playing
on the hard earth. And they were shut in like a barracks
enclosure, very strange.

Even fifty years ago the squares were unpopular. It was

'common' to live in the Square. It was a little less common to live in the Breach, which consisted of six blocks of rather more pretentious dwellings erected by the company in the valley below, two rows of three blocks, with an alley between. And it was most 'common', most degraded of all to live in Dakins Row, two rows of the old dwellings, very old, black four-roomed little places, that stood on the hill again, not far from the Square.

So the place started. Down the steep street between the squares, Scargill Street, the Wesleyans' chapel was put up, and I was born in the little corner shop just above. Across the other side of the Square the miners themselves built the big, barn-like Primitive Methodist chapel. Along the hill-top ran the Nottingham Road, with its scrappy, ugly mid-Victorian shops. The little market-place, with a superb outlook, ended the village on the Derbyshire side, and was just left bare, with the Sun Inn on one side, the chemist across, with the gilt pestle-and-mortar, and a shop at the other corner, the corner of Alfreton Road and Nottingham Road.

In this queer jumble of the old England and the new, I came into consciousness. As I remember, little local speculators already began to straggle dwellings in rows, always in rows, across the fields; nasty red-brick, flat-faced dwellings with dark slate roofs. The bay-window period only began when I was a child. But most of the country was untouched.

There must be three or four hundred company houses in the squares and the streets that surround the squares, like a great barracks wall. There must be sixty or eighty company houses in the Breach. The old Dakins Row will have thirty or forty little holes. Then counting the old cottages and rows left with their old gardens down the lanes and along the twitchells, and even in the midst of Nottingham Road itself, there were houses enough for the population, there was no need for much building. And not much building went on when I was small.

We lived in the Breach, in a corner house. A field-path came down under a great hawthorn hedge. On the other side was the brook, with the old sheep-bridge going over into the meadows. The hawthorn hedge by the brook had grown tall as tall trees, and we used to bathe from there in the dipping-hole, where the sheep were dipped, just near the fall from the old mill-dam, where the water rushed. The mill only ceased grinding the local corn when I was a child. And my father, who always worked in Brinsley pit, and who always got up at five o'clock, if not at four, would set off in the dawn across the fields at Coney Grey, and hunt for mushrooms in the long grass, or perhaps pick up a skulking rabbit, which he would bring home at evening inside the lining of his pit-coat.

So that the life was a curious cross between industrialism and the old agricultural England of Shakespeare and Milton and Fielding and George Eliot. The dialect was broad Derbyshire, and always 'thee' and 'thou'. The people lived almost entirely by instinct, men of my father's age could not really read. And the pit did not mechanise men. On the contrary. Under the butty system, the miners worked underground as a sort of intimate community, they knew each other practically naked, and with curious close intimacy, and the darkness and the underground remoteness of the pit 'stall', and the continual presence of danger, made the physical, instinctive, and intuitional contact between men very highly developed, a contact almost as close as touch, very real and very powerful. This physical awareness and intimate togetherness was at its strongest down pit. When the men came up into the light, they blinked. They had, in a measure, to change their flow. Nevertheless, they brought with them above ground the curious dark intimacy of the mine, the naked sort of contact, and if I think of my childhood, it is always as if there was a lustrous sort of inner darkness, like the gloss of coal, in which we moved and had our real being. My father loved the pit. He was hurt badly, more than once, but he would never stay away. He loved the contact, the intimacy, as men in the war loved the intense male comradeship of the dark days. They did not know what they had lost till they lost it. And I think it is the same with the colliers of today.[10]

Coal was to nineteenth century Britain what oil, gas and electricity are to the twentieth — and more besides. Approaching its peak — but past its prime — in 1900 the industry was steam- and export-oriented. As the industry moved more and more on to the concealed fields the popular view was that Kent was the coalfield of the future and the view that its future might be at best difficult and uncertain was scarcely ventured. Many obscure fields survived, meeting local needs by simple methods, the vestiges of 1800 alongside giants of 1900.

IRON AND STEEL

Coal was the motive power of the nineteenth century; iron and later steel were the essential capital goods in such forms as rails and girders, steam engines, screws and eventually ships. To make these goods, coal and limestone were required as well as iron ore and for much of the century the presence of iron ores in the coal measures was an additional force drawing iron-making to the coalfields. Only in the last quarter of the century did imported and non-coalfield ores exert a strong locational influence. It is moreover in this period that the apparent fortunes of the two industries diverge: the export boom in the coal trade was accompanied by general stagnation, occasional sharp depression, and loss of overseas markets in the iron and steel industry. In general iron-making was subject to sharper fluctuations than the coal trade — Scottish pig iron for example fetched 116s per ton in 1873, 46s six years later. If opening an iron works was almost as speculative a venture as sinking a coalmine, the former could more easily be put back into production than an abandoned mine. By comparison with the coal trade some innovations, Nielsen's hot blast for example, were applied relatively quickly. From mid-century however the geography of the industry is more of opportunities rejected than seized, of changes resisted than welcomed (particularly in steel making) as well as of the gradual impact of the depletion of coal and associated iron reserves.

The iron industry expanded quite as remarkably as coal-mining. At the start of the century about a quarter of a million tons of iron were made each year, at its end about ten million (figure 14). An eightfold increase in output between 1830 and 1870 rather outstrips the contemporaneous upsurge in coal production. Moreover locational changes were more marked in the iron and steel industry, thus South Wales and the West Midlands made two-thirds of Britain's pig iron in 1800, whereas between them the north east, the north west, and Scotland

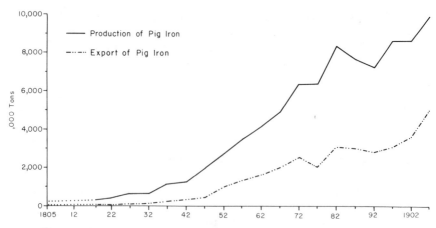

Figure 14. Britain's production and export of pig-iron 1805-1907. (Drawn from five-yearly data in Deane, P., and Cole, W.A., *British Economic Growth 1688-1959*, Cambridge, 1962, table 56.)

produced three-quarters of the iron and steel made in 1900 (figures 15 and 16).

The iron industry of the early nineteenth century occupied some of the best known sites of the Industrial Revelution — Coalbrookdale, Cyfartha, Carron, for example. These were centres of both coal and ore production, and at this period smelting required twice as much coal as ore. During the Napoleonic war the demand for ordnance and the general economic buoyancy boosted the industry's contribution to gross national product to about six per cent; after the war it fell back to about three per cent, but at its peak in 1871 it exceeded 11 per cent. Early in the century many products of the mid-century boom scarcely existed: rails were a trivial concern, the demand was for steam engines, machinery, tools and hardware. Steel was as yet an expensive speciality, required mainly by cutlers and made in Sheffield by 'small scale concerns in the backyards and orchards of the houses of the town'.[11] In South Wales and the West Midlands however iron was big business, albeit already in decline in the more remote Shropshire. A typical early nineteenth-century iron enterprise might be made up of two or three blast furnaces, several coal and iron pits, a refinery, forge, puddling furnace, hammer and rolling mill; a degree of integration and the significance of late eighteenth-century inventions are apparent. By the middle of the 1840s Dowlais

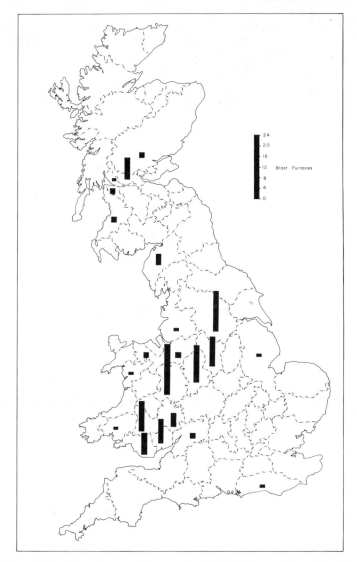

Figure 15. Britain's iron industry in 1796 (Redrawn from Roepke, H.G., *Movements of the British iron and steel industry 1720-1951, Illinois Studies in the Social Sciences,* 36, Urbana, 1956, p.25).

had 7,300 employees and was using 1,200 tons of coal to make 1,600 tons of iron each week, but already South Wales and the Midlands were losing at least their relative importance. Ore was becoming scarce in the latter, coal was to prove a more attractive investment in the former. Scotland had made only five per cent of Britain's iron in 1830; it made 16 per cent in 1839, and 29 per cent in 1852.

The basis of this success was Nielsen's hot blast process of 1828; resisted by some English ironmasters it was used in every Scottish works by 1835. Even the conservative Black Country was thoroughly converted by mid-century. Not only were there huge fuel savings, already discussed, but Scottish 'splint' coal could replace coke, and hitherto unusable Scottish black-band ores could be exploited. These savings, these low costs rather than high quality were the basis of Scottish dominance in the middle decades of the century. The most rapidly developing markets, the railways, wanted cheap iron rails in bulk rather than a quality product. The main centres of the industry were Monklands (plate 8) and Coatbridge, mining centres east of Glasgow linked to the sea by canal and railway, but other Scottish coalfields participated in the industry especially after

Figure 16. Britain's iron production 1796-1913: 1, other areas; 2, Lincolnshire and Northants; 3, Cumberland and Lancashire; 4, Derbyshire; 5, Northumberland, Durham and North Riding; 6, West Riding; 7, Scotland; 8, Shropshire; 9, Staffordshire (including Shropshire from 1905); 10, South Wales.

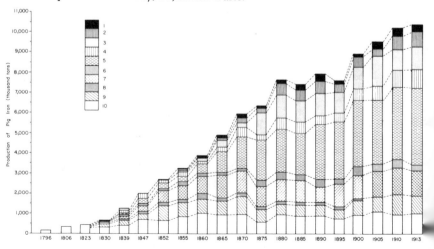

1845. Demand was universal, overseas as well as in Britain, and rails were to the iron trade what steam coal was to the coal trade; to an increasing extent heavier and tougher rails were required. By the 1850s iron rails exported to the U.S.A. were more valuable than cottons or woollens, but inevitably there was also an excess capacity and occasional acute depression. Moreover from 1850 new areas were entering the industry, notably the north-east coast on the basis of Cleveland ironstone and Durham coal. Middlesborough lit its first furnace in 1851, Teesside had 122 by 1871, when the region as a whole made one-quarter of Britain's iron and steel. This shift was largely a response to increased raw material problems in established areas, not felt in Scotland however until the last quarter of the century, and to a constantly improving technology which used less coke. The north-east coast had cheap, albeit low quality ores, and was close to the Durham coalfield; its coastal location was favourable to exports (and a growing shipbuilding industry). It could afford to be wasteful: 'commercial success in spite of wasteful methods [was] . . . a measure of the strength of her raw material resources'.[12]

The major element in the changing geography of the industry in the later nineteenth century is not however the location of new or old indigenous raw materials. It is the creation of a new product — steel — by a new technology and the problems of its adoption and implementation. The Bessemer Converter of 1856 and the Siemens Open-Hearth Furnace of 1868 made steel nearly as cheap as iron and in the long run a better bargain as it was more durable. The cutler's costly raw material became the 'ubiquitous source of strength for the architect, the engineer, the shipbuilder and armaments manufacturer'.[13] Unfortunately the quality of the new material, Bessemer steel in particular, was unreliable until late in the century, and expensive non-phosphoric ores were essential until the Gilchrist-Thomas 'basic' process was developed in 1878.[14] This 'basic' steel also took some time to establish a sound reputation.

The Bessemer process was particularly associated with the ousting of the iron rail by more durable steel in the 1870s — here quality mattered less than price. The supply of ore (non-phosphoric haematite) came from Cumberland, and by 1890 one-fifth of Britain's iron and steel industry was located there on the one British ore field suitable for the new steel processes. Cumberland ore travelled by rail to Cleveland, where local ore was phosphoric, and similar ores imported from Spain served the South Wales industry. Not only was South Wales close to Spain, compared say with Scotland, but steam coal was an attractive return cargo, so the industry, dependent on imported ore, began to move to the coast. Open hearth steel was more important in shipbuilding (and thus in such areas as Scotland and the North east) on account of its higher and more consistent quality. Lloyds first accepted steel ships in 1877[15] and within a decade steel was the almost universal building material. However open hearth steel was not produced in larger quantities than Bessemer steel until 1894, the process having been constantly improved while Britain's Bessemer industry was allowed to become semi-moribund: 'the mid eighties were seminal years for the open hearth steel industry, they were climacteric for the Bessemer industry'.[16] Herein lay one of the problems of the industry in the export market and in its reputation. The Admiralty gave 'basic' (Gilchrist-Thomas) steel parity with 'acid' (open hearth) in 1887 but prejudice against the former remained, and the process accounted for only one-fifth of output in 1900. The argument that the basic process inherently offered more to European producers, Britain's competitors, contains some truth, but the limited growth of the 'basic' industry again bears witness to stagnation and inertia. Thus British steel, wedded to the more costly and less satisfactory Bessemer technology, lost ground as an export save in such new and specialised areas as Sheffield's alloy steels. The industry also failed to make full use of the Jurassic phosphoric ores of the East Midlands. The industry set up there in 1853, to some extent under the auspices of coal and iron companies based in old-established areas, was still of only secondary importance in 1900 and much of the ore that was produced travelled north to be smelted. A degree of geographical inertia accompanied technical stagnation.

It is easy to exaggerate the decadence of the industry in the last years of the century, particularly as an exporter. Britain still accounted for 61 per cent of world steel exports in 1900 compared to 75 per cent in 1870; but between 1875 and 1896 Britain passed from making 47 per cent of the world's pig iron and 40 per cent of its steel, to 29 per cent and 22 per cent. Even more striking changes came in the next decade when

British output grew by one-third, that of Germany doubled, that of the U.S.A. increased fourfold. This was to some extent inevitable: 'the fundamental steelmaking inventions had been made in this country and we benefited from the close juxtaposition of ore and coal and their proximity to the coast. Apart from these there were, by 1880, very few favourable factors'.[17] Overseas producers had their advantages to exploit, their tariff walls to erect. But there is evidence to suggest that recession, relative as it was, went further than can be explained in terms of inherent overseas advantage, of 'some degree of failure . . . in the appreciation of or welcome given to novel principles or in the mode of their application'.[18]

What of the social geography of the iron and steel industry in nineteenth-century Britain? As the geographical patterns of the coal and iron industries slowly diverged, towns of various sizes devoted primarily to iron and steel were created — among them Middlesbrough, Askam and Millom. But such towns were fewer than the single-minded coalmining communities; more often the iron and steel business was carried on alongside others which were favoured by its presence, such as a variety of engineering trades. In environmental terms iron and steel was every bit as unpleasant as coal; on the one hand new communities were created very quickly, with all the problems of low quality and unplanned housing, and on the other the manufacturing process was demanding of space and productive of noise, smoke, dust, and waste. Thus Wolverhampton Corporation threatened to sue the firm of Lysaght for pollution in 1892 and 1895, for which reason the firm moved to Uskmouth in 1896. It was also a damaging consumer of resources — the Whitby ironstone mines for example were marked by 'refuse . . . brought out and deposited on the surface accumulating immense heaps of spoil, damaging and disfiguring the land upon which it was deposited'.[19] In Northamptonshire however it was only when the steam navvy replaced the pick and shovel, enabling deep deposits to be worked, from about 1895 that ironstone mining became seriously destructive of farm land.

At its peak in 1871 the industry, most broadly defined, employed 40 per cent of the adult male labour force, used 25 per cent of static steam power, and accounted for 11 per cent of gross national product. Mid-Victorian supremacy is epitomised in iron and steel; so, regrettably, is mid-Victorian complacency. Thus the industry manifested problems which have since become commonplace, and which worried some contemporaries, earlier than its peers: an indifferent export performance in a competitive situation, an excess of obsolete plant, an optimistic — at worst thoughtless — preference for the traditional and accepted over the innovational and radical. South Wales epitomises the geographical experience, continuity on old inland sites generating socio-economic problems only partly solved by a continuing transfer of the industry to coastal sites suitable for ore import.

NOTES

1 Young, Arthur, *Tours in England and Wales*, 1791, p. 275.
2 Lewis, E.D., *The Rhonnda Valleys*, London, 1959, p. 15; quoting Cliffe, C.F., *The Book of South Wales*, London, 1847.
3 Taylor, A.J., 'Combination in the mid-nineteenth century coal industry', *Transactions of the Royal Historical Society* (fifth series), vol. 3, 1953, p.23.
4 Machine cutting developed first on the older fields and thinner seams, not as Jevons suggests (*The British Coal Trade*, London, 1915, p. 211) in the Midlands. See Duckham's introduction to the 1969 edition, p.x.
5 The result of a famous accident at Hartley Colliery in Northumberland when the beam of the engine broke and blocked the one shaft, preventing access to trapped miners.
6 Taylor, A.J., 'Labour productivity and technological innovation in the British coal industry 1850-1914', *Economic History Review* (second series), vol. 14, 1961, p. 65.
7 Jevons, W.S., *The Coal Question*, London, 1865 (1st edition), p. 349. (The closing sentence of the book, Jevons' italics.).
8 The phrase was used in advertising coal from this New Zealand field. H.M.S. *Calliope* alone among seven naval vessels escaped from Apia, Samoa, during a hurricane in 1889. Her escape owed something to the quality of the coal; at the height of the storm her engines, usually capable of maintaining 15 knots, were able to sustain no more than half a knot into the teeth of the gale.

9 Campbell, R.H., 'The iron industry in Ayrshire', *Ayrshire Collections*, vol. 7, 1966, p. 100.
10 Lawrence, D.H., 'Nottingham and the mining country', in *Selected Essays*, London (Penguin), 1950 et seq., pp. 114-17. I am grateful to Dr G.C. Wynn for drawing my attention to this passage.
11 Birch, A., *The Economic History of the British Iron and Steel Industry 1784-1879*, London, 1967. p. 309.
12 Burn, D.L., *The Economic History of Steel Making 1867-1939: a Study in Competition*, Cambridge, 1940. p. 6.
13 Birch, A., op.cit., p. 315.
14 This lined the furnace with chemically 'basic' materials, generally limestones, to neutralise the phosphoric acids. The resultant basic slag turned out to be a valuable artificial fertiliser, rich in phosphorus.
15 Birch, A., op.cit., p. 362.
16 Sinclair, W.A., 'The growth of the British steel industry in the late nineteenth century', *Scottish Journal of Political Economy*, vol. 6, 1959, p. 44.
17 Burnham, T.H., and Hoskins, G.O., *Iron and Steel in Great Britain 1870-1930*, London, 1953, p. 266.
18 Burn, D.L., op.cit., p. 64.
19 Hoskison, T.M., 'Northumberland blast furnace plant in the nineteenth century', *Transactions of the Newcomen Society*, vol. 25, 1945-7, pp. 77-8.

FURTHER READING

1 COAL
Birch, T.W., 'The development and decline of Coalbrookdale coalfield', *Geography*, vol. 19, 1934, pp 114-26.
Crowe, P.R., 'The Scottish Coalfields', *Scottish Geographical Magazine*, vol. 45, 1929, pp 321-36.
Galloway, R., *A History of Coal Mining in Great Britain*, 1882 (reprinted with an introduction by B.F. Duckham, Newton Abbot, 1969).
Green H., 'The Nottinghamshire and Derbyshire coalfield before 1850', *Journal of the Derbyshire Archaeological and Natural History Society*, vol. 56, 1935, pp.44-60.
Holmes, W.D., 'The Leicestershire and South Derbyshire coal-

field', *East Midland Geographer,* vol. 10, 1958, pp.16-26.

Jevons, H.S., *The British Coal Trade,* London, 1915 (reprinted Newton Abbot, 1969).

Jevons, W.S., *The Coal Question . . . the probable exhaustion of our coal mines,* London (1st edition), 1865.

Jones, P.N., 'Colliery settlement in the South Wales coalfield', *Hull University Occasional Papers in Geography,* vol. 14, 1969.

Lawrence, D.H., 'Nottingham and the mining country', *in Selected Essays,* London (Penguin), 1950 et seq.

Lebon, J.H.G., 'Development of the Ayshire coalfield', *Scottish Geographical Magazine,* vol. 49, 1933, pp.138-53.

Lewis, E.D., *The Rhonnda Valleys,* London, 1959.

Morris, J.H., and Williams, L.J., *The South Wales Coal Industry 1841-75,* Cardiff, 1958.

Taylor, A.J., 'The Wigan Coalfield in 1851', *Transactions of the Historical Society of Lancashire and Cheshire,* vol. 106, 1954, pp.117-26.

Taylor, A.J., 'Labour productivity and technical innovation in the British coal industry 1850-1914', *Economic History Review,* (2nd series), vol. 14, 1961, pp.48-70.

Taylor, A.J., 'Combination in the mid-nineteenth century coal industry', *Transactions of the Royal Historical Society* (fifth series), vol. 3, 1953, pp.23-40.

Thomas, D.A., 'The growth and direction of our foreign trade in coal', *Journal of the Royal Statistical Society,* vol. 66, 1903, pp.439-522.

2   IRON AND STEEL

Beaver, S.H., 'The development of the Northamptonshire iron industry 1851-1930', in Stamp, L.D., and Wooldridge, S.W., *London Essays in Geography,* London, 1951, pp.33-58.

Birch, A., *The Economic History of the British Iron and Steel Industry 1784-1879,* London, 1967.

Burn, D.L., *The Economic History of Steelmaking,* Cambridge, 1940.

Burnham, T.H., and Hoskins, G.O., *Iron and Steel in Great Britain 1870-1930,* London, 1943.

Campbell, R.H., 'The iron industry in Ayshire', *Ayrshire Collections,* vol. 7, 1966, pp.90-102.

Carr, J.C., and Taplin, W., *A History of the British Steel*

Industry, London, 1962.

Flinn, M.W., and Birch, A., 'The English Steel Industry before 1856', *Yorkshire Bulletin,* vol. 6, 1954, pp.163-77.

Gale, W.K.V., *The Black Country Iron Industry,* Newton Abbot, 1966.

Harris, A., 'Askam iron: the development of Askam-in-Furness, 1850-1920', *Transactions of the Cumberland and Westmorland Antiquarian and Archaeological Society,* vol. 65, 1965, pp.381-407.

Harris, A., 'Millom: a Victorian new town', *Transactions of the Cumberland and Westmorland Antiquarian and Archaeological Society,* vol. 66, 1966, pp.449-67.

Lord, W.M., 'The development of the Bessemer process in Lancashire 1856-1900', *Transactions of the Newcomen Society,* vol. 25, 1945-7, pp.163-80.

Roepke, H.G., 'Movements of the British Iron and Steel Industry 1720 to 1951', *Illinois Studies in the Social Sciences,* vol. 36, 1956.

Scrivenor, H., *History of the Iron Trade,* London, 1841 et seq., (reprinted London, 1967).

Sinclair, W.A., 'The growth of the British steel industry in the late nineteenth century', *Scottish Journal of Political Economy,* vol. 6, 1959, pp.33-47.

Warren, K., *The British Iron and Steel Sheet Industry since 1840,* London, 1970.

Warren, K., 'Locational problems of the Scottish iron and steel industry since 1760', *Scottish Geographical Magazine,* vol. 81, 1965, pp.18-36 and 87-103.

Warren, K., 'The Sheffield rail trade 1861-1930: an episode in the locational history of the British steel industry', *Institute of British Geographers: Transactions,* vol. 34, 1964, pp.131-57.

Wilkins, C., *The History of Merthyr Tydfil,* Merthyr Tydfil, 1867.

4 Cotton and Wool: The New Staple and the Old

COTTON

Cotton was the most important of the great consumer-oriented industries of the nineteenth century; it is also often regarded as occupying a very central position in the Industrial Revolution on account of the rapidity of its growth and the novelty and distinctiveness of its economic organisation (plates 9 and 10). Its historical geography is both simpler and more complex than that of the coal and iron trades. Localisation was carried to extremes — at the end of the nineteenth century the main secondary centre of the industry, around Glasgow, employed little more than one-twentieth the number of hands of the Lancashire industry. Why this should be so is not entirely clear. It was in part the result of a mixture of geographical advantage and chance circumstance operating in the last decades of the eighteenth century and the first of the nineteenth. Furthermore there was extreme specialisation both in the extent to which communities depended on the fortunes of their mills, and in the development of a high degree of local specialisation within the industry. As with coal however growth was no simple and speedy adoption of new technologies but rather their gradual evolution in an often quite conservative and labour intensive business looking for a large share of its profits in overseas markets.

A concentration of the industry around Manchester was evident by the end of the eighteenth century. Here spinners were already showing a preference for coalfield sites for their factories although water power had done much to mould the industry's geography and weaving was still a dispersed domestic trade in the absence of looms suitable for factories. As yet North America supplied only about one-quarter of imported cotton, but by the 1830s it was supplying four-fifths, a dependence which continued, not always to Lanceshire's advantage, through the rest of the century. By 1802 cotton made up between four per cent and five per cent of Britain's gross national product, by 1812 (having overtaken wool) between seven per cent and eight per cent. Exports were basic to the industry: 'the tentacles of the Manchester trade reach out to all corners of the world, and whatever form of manufactured cotton is sought. . . someone can be found in Manchester ready to accept a commission'.[1] Moreover the cotton trade brought foreigners to Manchester, perhaps most notably Friedrich Engels.[2] Only rarely was less than half the output exported, usually by the end of the century four-fifths. Cotton cloth went to China, India and the tropics,[3] and also, early in the century, to Europe and the U.S.A. As these latter developed their own manufacture their importance as export markets diminished, but Europe remained a market for yarn. On this basis the British industry grew from a consumption of 60 million pounds of cotton in 1800 to use over 1,300 million pounds by the 1880s (figure 17). It employed half a million people and controlled almost three-quarters of the world's trade in cotton goods at the end of the century.

Such growth justifies Armitage's use of the word 'procession' to characterise the industry,[4] a procession occasionally and ephemerally interrupted by such crises as the scarcity of raw materials during the American Civil War. But as a procession moves on so did the industry reorganise its geography — Lancastrian pre-eminence was enhanced, regional specialisation became more marked, the industry as a whole adjusted its location remarkably closely to that of the coalfields. And yet the pre-eminence of Lancashire remains something of a mystery: evidently it is related to the rapidity of the early growth of the industry, to the proximity of coal and water power, to the port of Liverpool, perhaps to entrepreneurial traditions and to the Napoleonic War. Why did the industry not thrive in some similar west coast coalfield, Cumberland or Bristol for example, in certain respects seemingly more favourable than the margins of the Pennines for the export processing of imported raw materials? It remains the case, as Deane wrote in 1965, that 'it is not entirely clear why it should have been so concentrated in Lancashire'.[5]

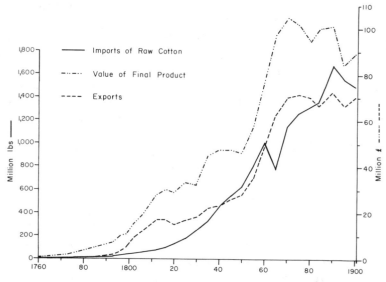

Figure 17. Imports of raw cotton, exports of cotton products, and their value 1760-1901. (Drawn from Deane, P., and Cole, W.A., *British Economic Growth 1688-1959*, Cambridge, 1962, tables 42-3.)

The question of functional specialisation — weaving in the north, spinning in the south — has likewise been no more than partly solved, and until recently has often been overshadowed by the parallel, and dramatic, issue of the plight of the handloom weaver when machinery was adopted in this part of the industry. This too was a geographical phenomenon: 'a good many problems of the weavers stemmed from the fact that the early distribution of factories in general did not always correspond to the still earlier distribution of the hand-loom weavers'.[6] Work was not where the weavers were. A third related issue is the very early development of local special-isation, Bolton's concern with fine spinning and Rochdale's with coarse for example. Nevertheless the basic problem is that of the emergence by mid-century of a weaving north and a spinning south separated by upland Rossendale.

Domestic cotton spinning and weaving had often been carried on under the same roof and although domestic weaving survived until mid-century its migration to factories from the 1820s was often to concerns already active in spinning. A Lancashire witness before a House of Commons Select Committee in 1833 observed that at that date all new spinning mills had weaving sheds attached. These 'combined firms' were the norm for the industry at this period, reaching their zenith in mid-century. Early investment in power looms was in fact often financed from the profits of spinning and thus occurred in the established spinning towns, such as Bolton and Bury. The geographical separation of weaving and spinning began only in the 1840s; new weaving enterprises were set up in such northern towns as Blackburn and Burnley. In part this was a result of the economics of increased specialisation in a growing industry, but it also reflected a divergence in the commercial needs and attitudes of each branch of the industry. The weaver's business was the more risky in the size and variety of stocks which had to be held and successful management seems primarily to have been a matter of matching order book and output. This required constant attention to detail and kept firms relatively small. Association with a spinning mill ceased to be advantageous. What attracted weavers to the north from the 1840s was cheaper labour, in the absence of factory spinning, coal, and improved rail access. The spinner's business was more certain and straightforward allowing considerable scale economies and thus the early development of the large joint-stock company. There was no reason for such firms to go north, to leave the established spinning district and its reservoir of skills and contacts. Thus while the combined firm remained common, by 1884 62 per cent of looms were in the north, 78 per cent of spindles in the south (figure 18).

The close geographical correspondence of coalfields and cotton manifests the industry's increasing dependence on steam, and the desirability of a local supply of coal in the period before the railways were built. Not only was the period prior to about 1840 one of rapid growth in the trade but also of easily accessible local coal and very inefficient — and thus coal-demanding — steam engines. Dependence on coal rather than running water meant a spatially contracting industry, particularly from the steepest and remotest valleys; it was also a further factor removing the size constraint and making possible larger units of production, bigger mill towns. The concentration of weaving into such towns as Burnley is the extreme case of this geographical trend, the dispersed domestic industry re-

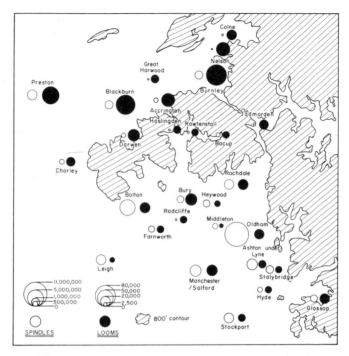

Figure 18. Looms and spindles in Lancashire, 1901 (Drawn from data in *Encyclopaedia Brittanica*, 1910 edition, Vol. 7, p.288).

placed by the steam-powered factory centred on coal. By 1900 a third geographical element had appeared, the decline of Manchester as a manufacturing centre and its concentration on an administrative and commercial role, perhaps a result of the position attained by the limited liability company in the industry by this date. The situation was not however without its anomalies: why did Preston, not on the coalfield, attract cotton? is the substitution of cheap labour and food for cheap coal in one of the county's chief market towns a convincing explanation? what part did the mid-century development of a dense railway network in the county play? The industry's failure to develop on the coalfield at St Helens represents the converse situation — a function of pollution created by the chemical manufactures?

By 1840 'cotton manufacture had already taken up a geography which differed only in detail from the present day'.[8] This is perhaps an exaggeration, particularly with respect to the northern cotton towns, but certainly youth had passed almost prematurely into middle-aged prosperity; the great investment phase of 1830-45 had laid down the industry's geography on the coalfields just before the railways began to create a close-knit and efficient communications network. The pattern was to be transformed only by worldwide economic and political changes after 1918.

COMPARISONS

Cotton, coal and iron are commonly regarded as the heartland of the nineteenth-century economy, thus some comparison is apt before the great traditional staple — wool — is examined. Had the years of maximum contribution to gross national income of the three industries coincided — which they did not — they would have contributed about one quarter of that income. Their role was pivotal in this sense, and in a second sense in the dependence of almost every branch of industry on coal and iron. It is, however, unreasonable to estimate the health or character of nineteenth-century Britain on the basis of these industries alone, witness Wilson's examination of the 'depression' of the last quarter of the century, an experience primarily of the iron and steel industry and of agriculture. In fact of coal, iron and cotton, all three export-oriented industries, only one was in some sense depressed by 1900. Other parallels present themselves; in each there was a gradual movement away from a propensity to innovate towards technological conservatism. These great labour-saving industries are by the end of the century the great capital-saving industries. Locational conservatism develops even earlier, favoured by the extent of their growth before the railways were built; these served to maintain a geographical *status quo* rather than to allow the development of new sites, even in the iron and steel industry where there was considerable technical progress and stimulus to movement after the railways came. Why no second or third 'Lancashire'? Why the limited development of the iron trade on the Jurassic ore-fields? Geographical lethargy belongs with entrepreneurial shortcomings — of which it is one facet — and technical conservatism in explaining eventually effective overseas competition. Coal necessarily escapes this criticism to some degree, although its reluctance to mechanise should be recalled, and it certainly shared the acute problems of cotton and iron after 1918. The three industries created a substantial portion of the new settlement geography of nineteenth-century Britain, a geography of single-industry communities, of mile upon mile of brick or stone terraces climbing out of the smoky valleys up the hillsides or spreading shapelessly across the plains.

Houses, derelict land, perhaps even a frame of mind, are their legacies to the last quarter of the twentieth century. The industries themselves, cotton and coal in particular, are ghosts by comparison with nineteenth century gigantism. They have experienced almost unceasing problems since 1918. But it is these industries which led Britain's socio-economic transformation and created some of its most characteristic landscapes during the nineteenth century, making Britain as much a New Society as America was a New World. What role then did the older and more conservative industries, wool for example, and new mass-production consumer-oriented industries play in that New Society?

WOOL

The nineteenth-century transformation of Britain's wool manufacture[10] presents some parallels with cotton; there was a high degree of concentration into one coalfield and intensely localised specialisation within that area. But in most respects the woollen industry was quite a different phenomenon. Traditionally the pre-eminent British manufacturing industry it was relatively in decline during this period and its contribution to the national income shrank from over four per cent in the 1820s to only one and half per cent in 1900. Never more than half of total output, more often only one-quarter or one-third, was exported; a sevenfold expansion of raw material consumption, a threefold increase in the value of the end-product is modest by Lancashire standards (figure 19). From about 1850 the industry generally employed somewhere between 250,000 and 300,000 workers, half the number at work in the cotton industry. Ironically the wool industries have survived the stresses and strains of the twentieth century rather better than their youthfully more vigorous trans-Pennine neighbour.

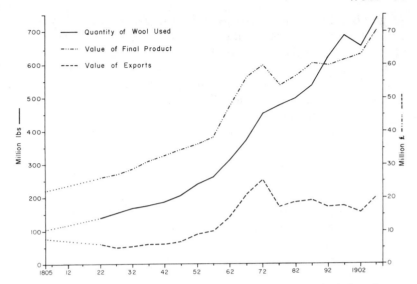

Figure 19. Wool use, export of wool products, and their value 1805-1908 (Drawn from Deane, P., and Cole, W.A., *British Economic Growth 1688-1959*, Cambridge, 1962, table 47).

The pre-eminence of the West Riding in the wool industry dates from the nineteenth century when its ancient and established rivals, Norfolk and the West of England, almost completely gave up the business. Yorkshire never achieved as complete a dominance of wool as did Lancashire of cotton; nevertheless by 1850 the West Riding contained 87 per cent of all worsted spindles and 95 per cent of worsted looms, and Yorkshire and Lancashire (where there were important outliers of the industry) possessed 87 per cent of all woollen spindles and 95 per cent of woollen looms. Only in the Tweed valley, and on a much smaller scale, was there dynamism and momentum in wool comparable to that of the West Riding.

How did this happen? Yorkshire's medieval woollen industry and the rather later worsted industry both grew rapidly during the eighteenth century; the output of broadcloth increased more than sixfold between 1726 and 1790. 'There is not I believe any reason to seek novel causes explanatory of the first rise of Yorkshire. It is the ordinary case of a pushing, hardworking locality, with certain slight advantages, attacking the lower grades of an expanding industry.'[11] The proverbially active and aggressive Yorkshireman is a factor in historical geography. Clapham's analysis has been criticised on points of detail, but majority opinion shares his view that an explanation of Yorkshire's success is to be found more in temperament and tactics than in locational advantage. The conservatism of East Anglia in particular, shared to a considerable degree by the West of England, was a great liability: 'geography alone does not explain the fact that it was more than a generation before the first mill engine was set going in Norwich'[12] (in 1838). Possibly Yorkshire's principal advantage was proximity to Lancashire and, thus to a whole series of late eighteenth- and early nineteenth-century innovations in textile technology which, with suitable modifications, were applicable to wool; there is certainly ample evidence for their diffusion across the Pennines. Coal, relatively abundant in the West Riding, became important only at a later stage — and Tweedside is remote from the coalfields. Part of the domain of the old West of England industry is not.

The two principal elements in the triumph of the West Riding remain matters of entrepeneurial choice: a concentration on the cheaper and coarser end of the market, and thus in the nineteenth century a larger and more readily expanded one, and the early introduction of machinery in the face of technical problems and an unwilling labour force.[13] On the whole it was more difficult to use steam or water driven machinery in the wool industry than in the cotton trade; this was particularly true of woollens where the power loom ousted the hand loom only in mid-century, and where as late as 1856 only half the labour force worked in factories. The West of England and East Anglia stuck to quality and mechanised tardily; as a worsted producer dependent on yarn produced in the West Riding the latter was particularly vulnerable. Moreover cotton was a competitor of some worsteds in the first part of the century. Neither area possessed the dynamism, the fashion sense, or the good fortune of the Tweed mills. Fashion and quality were in fact an integral and permanent problem for so diverse and many sided an industry as wool manufacture: 'there is nothing in the woollen or worsted trade comparable to the demand for plain cotton goods from India and the tropics'.[14] Worsteds in turn faced competition from cottons and from fashion-conscious — even fashion-forming — French weavers. Woollen manufacturers saw their fashionable broadcloths fall into disfavour and there were also prohibitive tariffs, notably in the U.S.A., after mid-century. But as there were problems so there were solutions, a greater emphasis on home markets, the export of worsted yarn rather than fabric, the creation of new materials. In some of these latter the West Riding was never seriously challenged — shoddy was a creation of the first half of the nineteenth century around Batley and Dewsbury for example.

What was the geographical character of this newly pre-eminent industry? In the broadest sense it was contracting. Beverley and York had been medieval woollen towns but were so no longer; Lancashire woollen industry succumbed to cotton competition albeit with important exceptions such as Rochdale flannels and Rossendale felts. Within the West Riding some remote areas decayed — Penistone for example, in a locality oriented primarily towards Sheffield. With the successive concentration of the seemingly innumerable processes of the wool trade into factories the traditional dispersion of the industry diminished but it did not disappear; the process had begun with medieval fulling mills and ended in the second half of the nineteenth century with the factory weaving of woollen cloth. Two circumstances account for the continuance of dispersion and its effects on the location of factories. There were strong, centuries old, commercial links between the industry's commercial centres, like Halifax and Huddersfield, and numerous weaving-cum-farming hamlets. Moreover power weaving was a late arrival, in the woollen trade especially, coming after the development of the railway. Such operations as carding and spinning entered factories and migrated to the valleys early in the century, creating such new and character-istically named settlements as Brighouse and Meltham Mills; water power attracted them there but they soon turned over to steam and were well served by river, canal, and railway. Weaving, domestic and factory, kept to the hills, and by the time the power loom triumphed steam was the motive force and coal was widely, albeit not abundantly, available in the Millstone Grit and Lower Coal Measures of these areas.

Sigsworth, the historian of the worsted trade, aptly summar-ises this process:

'First woollen scribbling (one part of the carding process) and then spinning had been drawn down from the uplands into the valleys by the attractive force of water power to drive the new machines which were being introduced in the late eighteenth century. No similar innovation had been made in weaving where the handloom remained supreme until well into the nineteenth century, and weaving remained on the uplands. With the introduction first of the steam engine and then of the steam-driven power loom ease of access to adequate coal supplies began to influence the location of wool textile mills. Their continued existence on the upland or the successful conversion of an existing domestically organised upland weaving concern into a factory organisation depended on the ease with which coal could be obtained. Where coal was not easily accessible, weaving also migrated to the valleys where engines to drive power-looms could be supplied with coal brought by the canals and roads, and later the railways, which followed the valley floors: "if there was coal to be had near at hand the clothier who was employing many hand-loom weavers built a mill near his warehouse and introduced power-looms. It was the natural course, for his weavers were all round about on the uplands . . . But manufacturing i.e. weaving could only survive on the hills and in the old hill-top towns if coal could be obtained locally or could be brought economically."[1 5] (figure 20)

Thus arose the geographical amalgam of congested but accessible valleys and seemingly improbable hill-top textile communities such as Queensbury; by mid-century this geography had superimposed itself upon the old pattern of market towns and hamlets. The limits were set firstly by accessibility, notably for coal although wool did not follow the coal industry eastwards, secondly by competition from more dynamic industries, notably cotton, perhaps coal, and thirdly by historical accident, as Charlesworth was able to demonstrate on the industry's southeastern margin.

Within this geographical complex there existed and developed a high degree of geographical specialisation. Woollen and worsted manufacture are very different technologies using different raw materials. Worsted manufacture took more easily and speedily to cotton-derived technology than did woollens; thus geographical correlation with coal appears early in the

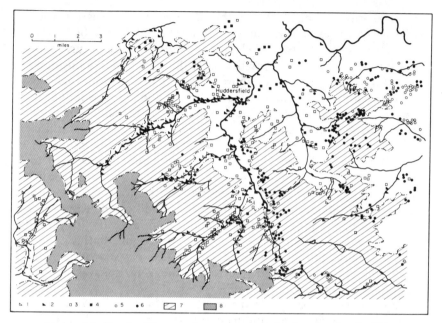

Figure 20. Wool mills, warehouses and coal mines in the Huddersfield district c. 1850: 1, disused mills; 2, mills in use; 3, disused warehouses; 4, warehouses in use; 5, disused mines; 6, mines working; 7, land between 600' and 1250'; 8, land over 1250'. (Redrawn from Crump, W.B., and Ghorbal, G., *History of the Huddersfield Woollen Industry*, Huddersfield, 1935, p.117.)

century, since steam-driven machinery was first used for this branch of the wool trade. Yarn of known quality could be purchased from spinners by weaving firms to produce a range of worsted fabrics. Traditionally Halifax had been Yorkshire's main worsted town but from late in the eighteenth century Bradford ousted its rival, mechanising more willingly and possessed of a better supply of coal. Between 1810 and 1830 Bradford's share of the drawback (rebate) paid to worsted manufacturers from the soap tax increased from 36 per cent of the total to 45 per cent, and by 1850 the city had almost half the county's worsted spindles and more than half the worsted power looms. It was the fastest growing of Yorkshire's large towns, its population increasing from 13,000 in 1801 to 103,000 in 1851. Woollen manufacture was — and is — a more complex process than worsted, and notably one in which the importance and variability of yarn quality is such as to favour vertical integration,[16] that is the one firm both spins the yarn and weaves it as well as carrying out other processes. Being less of a mass-production industry woollen manufacture was commonly carried on in smaller units than the worsted business. The trade comprised both the oldest part of the wool business — broadcloth — and the newest — shoddy and cheap woollens in general. The former, as in the West of England which it imitated, encountered problems during the century — fashion moved against broadcloth and the mass-market for expensive but durable cloths was limited. Woollen manufacturers had to diversify into a variety of new cloths known as 'fancy goods' (particularly on the coal measures where steam was cheap), into cheap cloth, or even into worsted. The shoddy trade was set up in 1813 and by 1858 Batley alone had at least fifty rag-shredding machines; the industry had filled the Batley valley and was spreading to Dewsbury and the Calder. Another area of growth, from the second quarter of the century, was carpet-making around Halifax.

Within the broad specialisation, Bradford and Halifax for worsteds, Leeds and Huddersfield (plates 11 and 12) for woollens, a high degree of local specialisation occurred, favoured in the latter instance by process complexity and product diversity. Within the heavy district for example Gomersal produced army and navy cloths, Earlsheaton blankets. As the period of most dynamic growth was mid-century, the early railway age, the final stages of movement into factories, so locational patterns and specialisations are of that period. The remarkably persistent geography of woollen and worsted Yorkshire is largely that set up in the middle decades of the last century.

Elsewhere, with one notable exception, the wool business was in decay. Tweedside was that exception. A remote low-quality industry whose production was valued at £26,000 in 1830 was transformed to a £200,000 a year industry by the late 1860s. A locale distant from coal, from markets, even from its main source of raw material, had succeeded by moving into the difficult 'quality' end of the industry. The basis of success was 'fundamental discoveries in the design of woollen cloth',[17] excellent market intelligence, and exploitation of the Victorian mania for Scott and the Scots. The Welsh industry, a possible and potential emulator of the Tweed, failed to follow its northern rivals to success, despite mechanisation and concentration into factories. Evidently Scottish flair for organisation and marketing were missing. The most successful Welsh mills were those of south-west Wales, often nineteenth-century railwayside creations, supplying flannels and blankets to the coalfield. Elsewhere many Welsh mills were extremely isolated, technically primitive, and dependent on local raw materials and markets.

Yorkshire's traditional rivals shared its early nineteenth-century war-based prosperity. Thereafter decline was almost continuous, and in the Norfolk case complete soon after mid-century. If decay was inevitable, disappearance was not: 'if Norfolk had taken full advantage of her opportunities she might conceivably have tided over that period in the early and mid-nineteenth century' — crucial for decaying as for developing industries — 'in which location was all important, diminished but not extinguished'.[18] Part of the West of England industry concentrated around Trowbridge and the Stroud Valley did survive, despite its failure to move out of broadcloths into a wider market. Worsted manufacture was the subject of some experiment, in mid-century of adoption, in the old serge-making region further west, but without much success. However an attenuated industry survived to enjoy some prosperity again in the twentieth century.

The geography of wool like that of cotton derives from past situations, from the changing transport and textile technology of the broad period 1775-1875, from the differing methods and organisations of the two branches of the industry, and from social, commercial, even ecclesiastical[19] circumstances which can be traced back into the Middle Ages. Cotton geography crystallises that of a relatively short period, the geography of wool a much longer time span, but in each case there is a notable correlation with accessible coal, a manifestation of the importance of the early nineteenth-century epoch of immobile steam. 'The historic textile towns . . . all lie on the Lower Coal Measures or within a mile or two either side of them, except Manchester and Wakefield. All but these two have within easy reach of them an area of Millstone Grit country where most of the weaving was done. They were the market towns, each for its own territory — the parish[20] (plate 13). The geography of the industry is thus as much of past patterns of buying and selling as of weaving and spinning.

NOTES

1 Copeland, M.T., *The Cotton Manufacturing Industry of the United States,* Cambridge, Mass., 1912, p.371. The statement neatly epitomises Manchester's role in the cotton industry almost from the start.

2 Engels worked in Manchester as agent for his father's Barmen cotton business in the early 1840s and *The Condition of the Working Class in England* (1844) is based on this experience.

3 The missionary with Bible in one hand, bale of cotton cloth in the other, is a stock — and almost comic — figure of school textbooks: his commercial importance for the cotton trade awaits investigation.

4 Armitage, G., 'The Lancashire cotton trade from the great inventions to the great disasters', *Memoirs and Proceedings of the Manchester Literary and Philosophical Society,* vol. 92, 1950-51, p.24.

5 Deane, P., *The First Industrial Revolution,* Cambridge, 1965, p.91.

6 Bythell, D., 'The handloom weavers in the English cotton industry during the Industrial Revolution: some problems', *Economic History Review* (2nd series), vol. 17, 1964-5, pp.345-6.

7 Discussed by Chapman, S.J., *The Lancashire Cotton Industry,* Manchester, 1904, p.163. The part played by 'accidental causes' is also admitted.

8 Rodgers, H.B., 'The Lancashire cotton industry in 1840', *Institute of British Geographers: Transactions,* vol. 28. 1960, p.136.

9 Wilson, C.H., 'Economy and Society in late Victorian Britain', *Economic History Review* (2nd series), vol. 18, 1965, pp.83-98.

10 A strict usage of the terms wool, woollen and worsted is adopted in this section. 'Wool' applies to the industry as a whole, 'woollen' to the production of cloth from carded fibres with some degree of felting, 'worsted' to the production of a fabric known variously as cloth or stuff from combed fibres with a minimum of felting.

11 Clapham, J.H., 'The transference of the worsted industry from Norfolk to the West Riding', *Economic Journal,* vol.

20, 1910, p.201.
12 Clapham, J.H., *Economic Journal*, vol.20, 1910, p.203.
13 One subject of Charlotte Brontë's novel *Shirley (1849)*.
14 Clapham, J.H., *The Woollen and Worsted Industries*, London, 1907, p.167.
15 Sigsworth, E.M., *Black Dyke Mills: A History*, Liverpool, 1958, pp.168-9.
16 There was no organised yarn market, as for worsteds, and since the quality of cloth largely reflected that of the yarn the weaver preferred to manufacture his own.
17 Stillie, T.A., 'The evolution of pattern design in the Scottish wool textile industry in the nineteenth century', *Textile History*, vol.1, 1970, p.310.
18 Clapham, J.H., *Economic Journal*, vol. 20, 1910, p.203.
19 Market centres such as Halifax and Huddersfield owed something to their role as centres — parish churches — for very large parishes comprising many wool-working villages and hamlets.
20 Crump, W.B., 'The wool textile industry of the Pennines in its physical setting', *Journal of the Textile Institute*, vol. 26, 1935, P.390.

FURTHER READING

1 COTTON

Baines, E., *History, Directory and Gazatteer* [sic] *of the County Palatine of Lancaster*, Liverpool, 1824-5 (reprinted Newton Abbot, 1968).

Blaug, M., 'Productivity of capital in the Lancashire cotton industry during the nineteenth century', *Economic History Review* (2nd series), vol.13, 1961, pp.358-81.

Bythell, D., 'The handloom weavers in the English cotton industry during the Industrial Revolution: some problems', *Economic History Review* (2nd series), vol.17, 1964, pp.339-53.

Chapman, S.J., *The Lancashire Cotton Industry: a study in economic development*, Manchester, 1904. (See also his article 'Cotton manufacture' in the 11th edition of *Encyclopaedia Brittanica*..)

Daniels G.W., *The Early English Cotton Industry*, Manchester,

1920.

Daniels, G.W., 'The cotton trade during the revolutionary and Napoleonic wars', *Transactions of the Manchester Statistical Society,* vol. 31, 1915-16, pp.53-84.

Edwards, M.M., *The Growth of the British Cotton trade 1780-1815,* Manchester, 1967.

Ellison, T., *The Cotton Trade of Great Britain,* London, 1886.

Jewkes, J., 'The localisation of the cotton industry', *Economic History,* vol. 2, 1930, pp.91-106.

Ogden, H.W., 'The geographical basis of the Lancashire cotton industry', *Journal of the Manchester Geographical Society,* vol. 43, 1927, pp.8-30.

Rogers, H.B., 'The Lancashire Cotton Industry in 1840', *Institute of British Geographers: Transactions,* vol. 28, 1960, pp.135-53.

Sandberg, L.G., *Lancashire in decline: a study in entrepreneurship, technology and international trade,* Columbus, Ohio, 1974.

Smelser, N.J., *Social Change in the Industrial Revolution, an application of theory to the Lancashire cotton industry 1770-1840,* London, 1959.

Shapiro, S., *Capital and the Cotton Industry in the Industrial Revolution,* Ithaca (N.Y.), 1967.

Taylor, A.J., 'Concentration and specialisation in the Lancashire cotton industry', *Economic History Review* (2nd series), vol. 1, 1949. pp.114-22.

Schulze-Galvenitz, G. von., *The Cotton Trade in England and on the Continent,* London and Manchester, 1895.

2   WOOL

Charlesworth, E., 'A local example of the factors influencing industrial location', *Geographical Journal,* vol. 91, 1938, pp.340-51.

Clapham, J.H., 'The transference of the worsted industry from Norfolk to the West Riding', *Economic Journal,* vol. 20, 1910, pp.195-210.

Clapham, J.H., *The Woollen and Worsted Industries,* London, 1907.

Crump, W.B., 'The wool textile industry of the Pennines in its physical setting', *Journal of the Textile Institute*, vol. 26, 1935, P.367-74 and P.383-94.

Crump W.B., and Ghorbal, G., *History of the Huddersfield Woollen Industry*, Huddersfield (Tolson Memorial Museum Publication, Handbook 9), 1935.

Edwards, J.K., 'The decline of the Norwich textile industry', *Yorkshire Bulletin*, vol. 16, 1964, pp.31-41.

Glover, F.J., 'The rise of the heavy woollen trade in the West Riding of Yorkshire in the nineteenth century', *Business History*, vol. 4, 1962, pp.1-21.

Heaton, H., 'Benjamin Gott and the industrial revolution in Yorkshire', *Economic History Review*, vol. 3, 1931, pp.45-66.

Jenkins, J.G., *The Welsh Woollen Industry*, Cardiff, 1969.

Jubb, S., *History of the Shoddy Trade*, London, 1860.

Lipson, E., *A Short History of Wool*, London, 1953.

Moir, E., 'Marling and Evans, King's Stanley and Ebley Mills, Gloucestershire', *Textile History*, vol. 2, 1971, pp.28-56.

Pankhurst, K.V., 'Investment in the West Riding wool textile industry in the nineteenth century', *Yorkshire Bulletin*, vol. 7, 1955, pp.93-116.

Ponting, K.G., *A History of the West of England Cloth Industry*, London, 1957.

Ponting, K.G., *The Woollen Industry of South-West England*, Bath, 1971.

Ponting, K.G. (ed.), *Baines's (1858) Account of the Woollen Manufacture of England*, Newton Abbot, 1970.

Sigsworth, E.M., *Black Dyke Mills: A History*, Liverpool, 1958. (Chapters 1 to 3 are a general history of the nineteenth century worsted industry.).

Sigsworth, E.M., 'Bradford and its worsted industry under Victoria 1837-1901', *Journal of the Bradford Textile Society*, vol. 59, 1952-3, pp.63-70.

Stillie, T.A., 'The evolution of pattern design in the Scottish wool-textile industry in the nineteenth century', *Textile History*, vol. 1. 1970, pp.309-31.

5 Manufacturers and Mass-Producers: The Geography of Necessities and Luxuries

Coal, iron, cotton and wool select themselves as major themes in the historical geography of nineteenth-century industrial Britain. Iron — or by the end of the century steel — provided the hull of the ship of state, coal was the driving force, cotton and wool exemplify new cargoes and old. Consideration of these realms is essential — a comprehensive survey of the other industries of the 'workshop of the world' is impossible. This chapter is then a choice and a selection, as much personal as rational: chemicals and paper represent existing industries which were transformed and which serviced a wide range of other industries and occupations, while brewing and milling were old and dispersed mass-consumption industries affected not only by steam but by government; the hosiery and the boot and shoe trades experienced the move from cottage to factory and in the latter case the rise of new methods of retailing.

CHEMICALS

The chemical industry was neither a huge producer, nor a great exporter, nor a large employer. In 1841 it employed less than one-twentieth of the labour force of the textile industries, and in 1901 still only one-fifth. In 1892 the Leblanc alkali trade in Widnes and Runcorn, one of the main nuclei of chemical manufacture, employed 1,100 specifically 'chemical' workers, aided by 5,000 general labourers. The interest and importance of the industry lies not its size but in that its growth was a prerequisite for more spectacular events elsewhere, in textiles and agriculture for example, and that its locational patterns were of such extreme variety and changeability. Entrepreneurial decision, raw material supplies, technological change, process linkage, and public pressure all played a part. Moreover the industry experienced both great success, in heavy inorganic chemicals, and catastrophic failure — after early pioneering — in some areas of organic chemistry.

Even in the relatively undeveloped chemical industry of the late eighteenth century the key role of sulphuric acid was evident, and Liebig's dictum that 'we may fairly judge of the commercial prosperity of a country by the amount of sulphuric acid it consumes'[1] retains much of its validity in the diversified chemical economy of the 1970s. The most direct, albeit not the most important, use of sulphuric acid at this period was as a bleach, a role it retained in a less direct form in the generation of sulphur dioxide for wool and silk, after bleaching powder came into use for cotton and linen early in the nineteenth century. The eighteenth-century alternatives, sour milk and sunlight, might well have placed severe constraints, locational as well as economic, upon the growth of the textile industries had there been no cheap sulphuric acid. Moreover the acid was also used to make chlorine and thus bleaching powder. The predominant use of sulphuric acid in the first half of the nineteenth century however was in the Leblanc process for soda (sodium carbonate) manufacture, the alkali industry as it was usually called. Devised in the 1790s it was a boom industry of the 1820s — soda was needed by soap makers, by glass makers, and to some extent for making bleaches. From the 1840s artificial fertiliser manufacturers were another important market for sulphuric acid.

Demand for sulphuric acid was thus widespread, but strongest in textile areas. The product was difficult, dangerous, and disagreeable to transport before the railways were built, but its manufacture by the lead-chamber process was simple and profitable, although imperfectly understood[2] and costly to establish. Only the raw materials presented problems. Sulphur was imported from Sicily until the 1840s when, for both political and economic reasons, pyrites from the coalfields and Spain was preferred. It is thus not surprising that even before the alkali boom the industry was dispersed. In 1830 there were 30 producers in Britain, of whom seven were in London, seven in central Scotland, four in Birmingham, three in Lancashire and three in Yorkshire. The surge in demand for alkali fostered the industry's growth, often as a subsidiary part of a Leblanc enterprise, but there were other linkages. As the industry turned to pyrites as a raw material, so copper smelting became associated with sulphuric acid manufacture, notably in South Wales and on Tyneside. And it was in part the copper industry of Tyneside which fostered the development of electrical engineering in that area late in the nineteenth century. A further cheaper and widely available source of sulphur became available and widespread in the 1870s, 'spent oxide' from gasworks. Thus an industry producing 10,000 tons per annum in the 1820s was producing 1,000,000 (a quarter of world output) by 1900; an essential chemical which had cost £30 to £35 a ton in the 1790s sold for 25s (£1.25) in 1885. By the end of the nineteenth century the catalytic contact process was replacing the lead chamber, and by its scale economies served to foster the localisation of a still very dispersed industry.

Sulphuric acid was only a beginning, an industry to meet the needs of other chemical manufacturers rather than the public at large. The main user was as has been mentioned the Leblanc soda maker who, in the early nineteenth century, was responding to a situation in which a surge of demand for his product outran the traditional vegetable (mainly kelp and barilla) source of supply. However the conservatism of users in the face of a synthetic product was one reason why Leblanc's idea of the 1790s took 30 years to become the basis of large-scale industry; the war and possibly the salt taxes (repealed in 1822) were also delaying circumstances. Not surprisingly those involved in trades killed by the new process (the barilla importers and the kelp interests in Scotland) also tried to delay its impact. In fact Britain's first small Leblanc industry appeared on Tyneside some time between 1802 and 1806; the process appeared at St Rollox, Clydeside (plate 13), a primarily entrepreneurial location,[4] only in 1818. Muspratt's Liverpool works of 1823 which later moved to St Helens was the first large-scale enterprise. By the 1830s the purer soda of Muspratt's Leblanc process was cheap enough and abundant enough to allow local soap producers to switch to palm oil, thus producing better soap and fostering Liverpool's tropical connections.

These three areas were to remain the heartland of the British inorganic chemical industry until late in the century. However

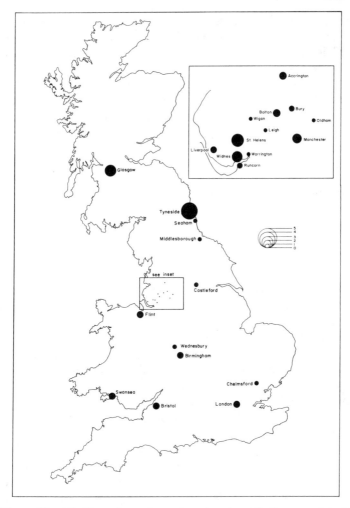

Figure 21. Alkali works registered under the Alkali Acts of 1863. (Drawn from data in Campbell, W.A., *The Chemical Industry*, London, 1971, table 12.)

the salt-coal axis of north Cheshire-south Lancashire linked by river, canal and railway was particularly important. In the two estuaries, Clyde and Tyne, chemicals were eventually over-shadowed by more conspicuous industries, notably shipbuild-ing, and St Rollox, although Europe's largest individual chem-ical works in the 1840s, suffered from remoteness from the major markets for bleaching powder and soda. Of 83 British Leblanc works listed in 1864 (figure 21), 36 were in Lancashire and 20 in the northeast. There were linkages inside the industry — colliers taking coal from the Tyne to the Mersey returned with Cheshire salt. Connections with local markets were strong in Lancashire and Cheshire, soap and bleach for cotton, soda for glass; elsewhere there were less immediately obvious connections. On Tyneside for example the soap industry owed something to coalmining, not however on account of demand among the miners but because the coal industry supported a candle industry and the soap industry used the softer tallows unsuitable for illumination. The wider implications must not be forgotten — cheap soap played an important part in the population explosion.

Until 1867 the Leblanc manufacturers, diversified as their interests often were into acid and bleach, reckoned to make their profits from soda. Exports were increasing (fivefold between the mid-fifties and mid-seventies) and 70 per cent of bleaching powder was exported to the U.S.A. in the 1870s, although as in so many other industries they were to run up against tariff walls by the end of the century. Tyneside was particularly associated with the export trade, and thus hard hit. However from the late sixties the Leblanc trade and its location changed rapidly. Hydrochloric acid, traditionally a waste product — a very noxious one — began to be used for chlorine generation, and the Alkali Acts of 1863, strictly limiting the acid's emission into the atmosphere, controlled technology and raised costs. The Solvay (Ammonia-Soda) process was establishing itself as the cheapest source of soda by the 1870s, forcing Leblanc producers to depend first on the chlorine and bleaching powder side of their trade and then, the price of now abundant chlorine proving so unremunerative, on copper recovery from the pyrites of their sulphuric acid plants for their profits. The Solvay process used brine rather than salt and less coal than the Leblanc system — Widnes alone had used a million tons of coal annually when its Leblanc industry was at its peak — and so the tendency was to move to the sources of brine and to larger works. The Tyne yielded to the Tees, the Weaver and Sankey to Northwich and Fleetwood. The United Alkali Company of 1890, a merger of Leblanc firms, had to rationalise in order to protect its interests, its very *raison d'être;* thus it quickly closed

20 out of 24 Tyneside works at the same time as it opened up the Fleetwood (Lancashire) salt field.

Alkali was not only the most important it was also the dirtiest and most damaging of the nineteenth-century chemical industries. The Leblanc process generated large quantities of hydrogen chloride gas which, being of no value at that period, was discharged into the atmosphere. The 1863 legislation insisted that no more than five per cent of the acid be allowed to escape, but the dilute acid discharged into rivers was almost equally unpleasant. The hallmarks of the industry were tall chimneys[5] to disperse the gas (plate 13), devastated vegetation, complaints, and law suits:

> 'the gas from these manufactures is of such a deleterious nature as to blight everything within its influence, and is alike harmful to health and property. The herbage of the fields in their vicinity is scorched, the gardens neither yield fruit nor vegetables; many flourishing trees have lately become rotten naked sticks. Cattle and poultry droop and pine away. It tarnishes the furniture in our houses, and when we are exposed to it, which is of frequent occurrence, we are afflicted with coughs and pains in the head'. (1839)[6]

The pollution problem drove Muspratt from both Liverpool and Newton-le-willows in 1849 and made Widnes in 1888 'the dirtiest, ugliest, most depressing town in England'.[7] The Alkali Acts could not reverse damage already done; moreover the industry produced and dumped a second, less dangerous but also less tractable by-product, the 'alkali waste' of calcium sulphide, calcium hydroxide, and coal. The waste tended to smoulder and in wet weather it gave off evil-smelling hydrogen sulphide. Chance's process for sulphur recovery from the 'alkali waste' tips came only in the 1860s after 40 years of accumulation and devastation.

The fertiliser industry, the creation of Leibig's method of superphosphate production in 1840, was basic to Britain's mid-century agricultural prosperity. The process used quite widely available materials — 'bones, bone ash, bone dust, and other phosphoric substances, mixing a quality of sulphuric acid just sufficient to set free such phosphoric acid as will hold in solution the undecomposed phosphate of lime'[8] — to serve a widespread market and was thus itself dispersed. Since bones were often imported coastal towns had some advantage; prizes for top quality superphosphate were awarded in 1881 to works as far apart as Plymouth and Inverness. It was an area of diversification for sulphuric acid makers — the Carnoustie fertiliser works of 1846 for example were an offshoot of St Rollox. Superphosphate manufacture was almost as unpleasant and un-neighbourly a business as the Leblanc trade and came under the control of the Alkali Acts in 1881; unfortunately the trade's characteristic — and even more offensive — associates, horse slaughtering, glue making, the knacker's business in general, did not. The ammoniacal by-products of coal-gas manufacture were another material for the fertiliser trade, and from the 1880s the iron and steel industry made its by-product contribution, basic slag.[9]

Organic chemicals however were one of the conspicuous failures of the nineteenth-century economy. An inability to exploit Perkin's discoveries, an inadequate base in chemical research and teaching, a high degree of dependence on German dyestuffs; this was the kind of commercial failure so frequently discussed in late Victorian Britain. Locationally these industries were footloose, employing such widely available materials as coal tar to make valuable end-products. Perkins set up his works at Harrow because he was a Londoner and the end-product of his process was able to withstand the cost of bringing benzene from Glasgow. The limited availability of technical education, save perhaps in agriculture, was one reason for the limited development of so technically sophisticated an industry; among others were ineffective patent laws, tariff problems, and difficulties with the Excise over the industrial use of alcohol. Dyes were the great failure — surprisingly so when textiles were such a thriving business — other areas less so. The explosives industry was one of the organic chemical industries which did well. The first British factory for organic explosives, built at Ardeer, Ayrshire, in 1871 (plate 14) occupied a classic site and location for so dangerous a trade, remote but with rail and water access to not too distant markets, the dunes facilitating the excavation of bunkers and the creation of embankments.

A note on the principal chemical reactions:

Lead Chamber Sulphuric Acid — in practice a simple process, but one of which the chemistry remains imperfectly understood. Sulphur and saltpetre (in proportions 7: 1) are burnt on trays in a lead-lined chamber, the floor of which is covered with water. Sulphur dioxide is produced, oxidised to sulphur trioxide which combines with water to produce sulphuric acid. Nitrogenous impurities are a problem, as also the time required for the process and the problem of making concentrated acid.

Leblanc Process — salt when heated with sulphuric acid produces hydrogen chloride (gas) and sodium sulphate. This sulphate is heated with limestone and coal to produce sodium carbonate (soda), calcium sulphide and carbon dioxide. The soda is dissolved out leaving the alkali waste which itself slowly produces hydrogen sulphide in the presence of water.

Solvay Process — a cold concentrated brine solution is saturated with ammonia and carbon dioxide producing ammonium bicarbonate. This reacts with salt to form ammonium chloride (from which ammonia is recoverable) and sodium carbonate, which excess carbon dioxide converts to the bicarbonate. This is insoluble in brine and is precipitated; heating decomposes it to the carbonate. Solvay's contribution was to make a profitable large-scale process out of a well known laboratory reaction.

Bleaching Powder — chlorine is passed over a layer of slaked lime (calcium hydroxide) in a lead or concrete chamber. The end-product, a mixture of calcium hypochlorite and basic calcium chloride, is an easily handled generator of chlorine, useful not only as a bleach but as a disinfectant.

PAPER MAKING

Paper making, like the chemical industry, was a small affair by comparison with textiles or mining, and yet its end product was used in almost every industry and played an integral part in the nineteenth century 'knowledge explosion'. In mid-century, on Coleman's estimate of a labour force of 43,000 people, the industry, broadly defined, employed about one-tenth the labour force of the coal industry, one-fifteenth that of textiles. Its role and status approximated to that of the chemical industry but as a technology it resembled textile manufacture, transforming natural products and wastes into a fabric rather than carrying out newly devised syntheses. As such it was as old established a trade as textiles.

The paper industry of 1800 was a handicraft industry, on the verge of the initial implementation of Fourdrinier's paper-making machine but with its widespread adoption still 30 years away. The basic raw material — rags — was widely available, albeit most readily in the cities and the textile and clothing districts.[10] The raw material supply situation was a perennial problem but was about to be eased by the use of bleaching powder and china clay to clean and add bulk to raw materials. The industry comprised many and widely scattered units, mostly small, rented from landlords and worked within a family or partnership organisation assisted by a small amount of hired labour.[11] The process of rag-pulping was mechanised and large quantities of water were used, hence stream-side locations were normal, often in mills which had begun — as they were to end — their working life in another trade. The working life of mills was often shortened by flood or fire, both particularly damaging and frequent in the paper industry. The growth areas of the early nineteenth-century industry were on the one hand its traditional centres, the Medway and the Chilterns, both of which had the advantage of being handy to London, and a similar market orientation south of Edinburgh; on the other hand the new industrial areas, notably Lancashire, at once a source of raw materials and a market. Other raw materials were also locationally significant, the 'old rope' of the maritime north-east coast, for example, a surprisingly common coastal cargo during the nineteenth century. The industry avoided remote areas, mid-Wales for example, since raw materials and end-product were bulky, and East Anglia, where the rivers were muddy and good sites for water mills relatively few (figure 22).

Mechanisation began in Hertfordshire and Huntingdonshire, but it favoured those areas well placed for coal, as well as a general increase in the scale of enterprise. Thus even before esparto grass in the 1850s and timber in the 1880s became important raw materials, remote inland sites were giving way to estuaries, the eastern margin of the Pennines to Yarm and Jarrow for example. By 1860 mechanisation had reduced hand-made paper to four per cent of an output which had

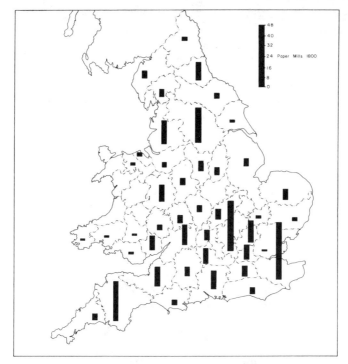

Figure 22. The paper mills of England and Wales, 1800. (Redrawn from Shorter, A.H., *Paper making in the British Isles*, Newton Abbot, 1971, figure 4).

increased sevenfold since 1800; moreover prices had halved. Some makers were vertically integrated, from stationery to rag collecting in a few cases, others horizontally, producing a wide variety of paper types. Cheap brown paper manufacture was more important on the coalfields and in the industrial areas where it was most in demand; quality white paper was more important around London and Edinburgh whose printers and publishers were its markets, and for the remote mills able to survive only by producing quality goods.

Markets, materials and tradition by no means exhaust a list of locational factors. Dickinson established esparto-based paper manufacture in Sunderland to avoid further water pollution in Hertfordshire. The abandonment of suitable buildings by other industries also provided a location for some paper makers. Lewis noted that in the water power period such circumstances

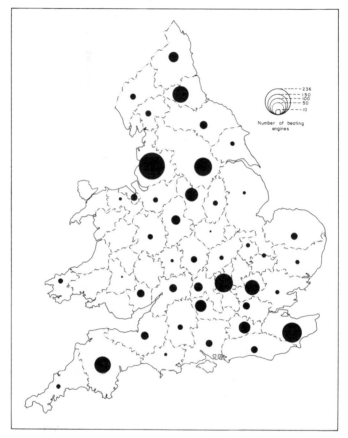

Figure 23. Paper mills (beating engines) in England and Wales 1911. (Redrawn from same source as figure 22, figure 14.)

favoured dispersion and facilitated the process of 'swarming' around an original mill, since water power limited mill size. Steam reversed this circumstance and favoured larger units. At a more local level he was able to show that in the Maidstone area mills using water from the Hythe aquifer were advantaged over others with a more ferruginous supply, but that narrow valley sites made expansion difficult and these mills thus tended to remain small and to specialise in high grade papers.

The rapid turnover to imported timber as the basic raw material in the last two decades of the century was seen as the final and complete solution to the raw material problem.

Market and material supply ceased to coincide geographically; the use of heavy inorganic chemicals (sulphates and sulphites) became a further locational factor favouring movement to the coast, already a well-established tendency. Areas such as the Medway and the north east were thus well placed for the timber-based industry, but it was able to remain powerful in Lancashire (figure 23). If the general tendency was for remote rural mills to disappear, the railway — and later the lorry — allowed prolonged survival in some such situations, Richmond (North Riding) and Witchampton (Dorset) for example. The pre-eminence of Kent and Lancashire was strengthened but the scattered and rural component and character survived.

BREWING

At the end of the eighteenth century the British spent more money on beer than on any other one item. Brewing could be at the one end of the scale a one-man or domestic business; at the other it could already be — as it generally was in London — big business. There were indeed considerable economies of scale, especially with the coming of steam power, but for these to be effected there had to be retail outlets, a matter of both availability and accessibility. Beer was a perishable and bulky product, and for ordinary beer in a horse and cart age the radius of distribution extended only from three to five miles from the brewery. In these circumstances urbanisation favoured the industrialisation of brewing. Its separation from retail selling has probably begun in London as early as the seventeenth century and by 1815 the 11 leading London brewers were producing 2,000,000 barrels a year, one-fifth of the nation's output. The best London beer, porter[12], enjoyed a wider market; it cost no more to ship a barrel of the very best than of the very worst beer, and it was by sea or canal that such beer travelled.[13] Generally the further one travelled from London, the coastal towns, and the best beers, the more frequently was the beer brewed very locally or even by the publican who sold it. In the highland zone not only was land transport more difficult and costly — to the domestic brewer's advantage — but another of his needs, fuel, was cheaper; moreover porter was still an innovation, and not to everyone's taste. London porter might, ironically, be sold in Dublin, but more generally local tastes, conservatism, and not least local pride favoured the local brewer, especially for everyday beer. Some centres outside London also enjoyed a more than local reputation. Burton upon Trent provides an example;[14] some of its finest beers could compete outside the vicinity of the town, but poor communications and the prevalent taste for porter impeded its growth: 'for centuries a great industrial potential there had lain imprisoned in a narrow overland marketing area by high transport costs until freed by the railway to Derby in 1839'.[15]

The railways allowed quality beer to be sold to a national market and Burton was aided in this respect by a move in public taste away from porter towards the light ales for which its hard water was so suited. Several London brewers migrated to Burton for this reason, Ind Coope in 1858 for example, or to similarly favoured hard water sites, as Courage to Alton. Existing breweries in such locations, as at Tadcaster, were given at least a regional advantage. The railway also generated a phase of public house relocation, away from turnpikes and canals to the 'Station'.[16] Nevertheless the greater part of the brewing business remained local and common beer was made by small brewers or by innkeepers in most areas outside London. In Leeds in 1851, possibly an extreme case, Tetley, the largest brewer, had a mere 32 employees — commercial brewers (as opposed to innkeeper-brewers) made only just over half the beer brewed in Britain. The average Leeds brewery of the mid-nineteenth century employed fewer than ten men. However by the end of the century the number of innkeeper-brewers had fallen to about ten per cent of the mid-century figure, and by 1914 47 large breweries produced 45 per cent of the nation's beer. Tetley was employing 400 men, but the average brewery still only a dozen or so. The stage had not been reached where brewing could cease to be dispersed, because of the limitations of horse and cart distribution, even though many company mergers had taken place. These were concerned more with marketing than with manufacturing, since assured retail outlets were essential for profitable brewing and these were to be found in 'tied' houses. This innovation also diffused outwards from London — half of London's pubs were 'tied' by 1815 — perhaps as part of the process whereby porter lost out to light ale and marketing became more competitive. There was also the question of the complex legal framework – and restrictions – imposed by parliament upon beer selling,[17] and of the capital needed by the retailer and most readily supplied by the brewer. In fact by the end of the century an outright scramble for licensed properties among brewers was adversely affecting profits, but a series and hierarchy of overlapping territories, each focused on a brewery, had been set up.

In 1900 brewing was still a dispersed activity, but more so with respect to plant than to company organisation. Although the family element was strong, even in the large companies, brewing was big business, witness the very scale of operation of the principal companies, their ownership of large numbers of public houses, and their backward integration into malt and hops. The even more radical impact of the motor lorry and van lay in the future.

FLOUR MILLING

The miller, like the brewer, was involved in the production of an everyday necessity, and like him he was to an increasing extent a wholesaler. The industry was geographically dispersed to meet demands for a bulky although not very perishable commodity and technologically conservative. If, as in the London breweries, steam had some impact before 1800, so in the 1830s and 1840s there were still disputes as to manorial rights over mills in Yorkshire.[18] Steam-powered mills became widespread in the first half of the nineteenth century, on the coalfields especially, but for each steam mill there were several water mills and an occasional windmill; the technology of the milling process itself remained medieval. As grain imports became more important and steam pre-eminent coastal locations were increasingly at an advantage and from mid-century millers began to experiment with roller methods, emulating their European (especially Hungarian) counterparts. By 1870 one firm of Liverpool millers had got rid of stones entirely, and it was from this centre and in the succeeding two decades that the large roller mill triumphed, aided by ever improving technology and the near-collapse of British grain farming. Circumstances favoured large coastal mills – Vernon's Birkenhead mill of 1898 (plate 15) had a 1,200 h.p. engine and produced 12,000 28 lb sacks of flour each week — while the old water mills (plate 16) decayed. Where milling was carried on inland the seat of business often shifted to the railway, at Cambridge from Newnham to a new enterprise at the station in 1900. The consumer was an unwitting — possibly willing — victim of progress since roller-milled flour was not only whiter, the popular preference, but often less nutritious. The ubiquitous trade of the early nineteenth century had become a localised, largely coastal, factory industry through the impact of steam, technology and foreign competition.

LEATHER

In 1800 the making of leather goods, and of leather itself, was the country's second largest manufacture. It was an ancient craft, carried on in almost every community, never wholly to lose this character but to be modernised and in many instances relocated, by chance and accident as well as by rational decision.

Tanning, fell-mongery and associated trades were in the early nineteenth century a small-scale, neighbourhood (albeit unneighbourly) activity. Markets and materials were almost universal although availability of the latter may in a few cases have initially favoured certain areas, oak-bark from Rockingham Forest the Northamptonshire leather trade for example. The main concentrations of the industry were near the ports where raw materials came in, at Bermondsey for example, and in areas concerned with leather manufactures like south Somerset. The tanner's trade was not liked by his neighbours,[19] hence the typical location at or beyond the edge of the town. During the century the small tanner tended to disappear, the business to concentrate on London, Leeds — the second largest centre by 1850 — and the ports. Communications mattered more than coal; movement to and from markets and sources of supply mattered more than fuel costs. British industry concentrated on heavy leathers, the lighter leathers were often imported; in general there was much inter-regional movement of the valuable end-product. In the 1860s Yeovil glovers bought leather from Northamptonshire whose bootmakers looked north and even overseas for their supply. As an historian of the county wrote in

1906 'the manufacture of leather . . . never attained to the importance which would be expected'.[20] After all the boot and shoe trade was but one market — heavy leather belting connected steam engine to machine and was thus integral to factory industry. Indeed it has been suggested that its importance was one reason for the industry's tendency to move north and for its neglect of light leathers. While technical changes were not a strong locational force — the industry was notoriously conservative, witness its reluctant adoption of the chrome process in 1884 — prolonged occupation of a particular site was not typical. The urban fringe was a moving frontier and this may in part explain why Northampton's 11 'heavy' tanneries of 1847 had all closed or moved elsewhere by 1906.

The principal leather-using industry was the manufacture of boots and shoes. At the beginning of the century this activity was widespread; Clapham estimated that in 1831 100,000 out of 130,000 bootmakers were local shopkeepers. The remainder, serving wider and more specialised markets, tended to be concentrated in a few provincial cities and towns. Some communities like Northampton had an association with the industry reaching back several centuries while in others it was, as a speciality, a comparatively recent arrival, at Stafford and Norwich for example. The industry was almost completely domestic, since cutting and warehousing alone could be centralised into factories. Most shoe-making processes came to be mechanised only in the 1850s and then with hand machines — steam power was an even later starter. More powerful elements in creating a factory system were compulsory education and extension of the Factory Acts to cover workshops in the 1870s, eliminating cheap labour and cheap premises. The unions and the manufacturers were equally keen to move the business into centralised establishments, the former the more readily to guard their members' rights and interests, the latter for the sake of quality control.

Geographical relocation on a nationwide scale began earlier than movement into factories. If the growth of the Northampton industry is the main feature of the first half of the nineteenth century, it was also during this period that Clarks of Street (Somerset) entered the trade (in the 1820s, at first as a sideline to their tannery and sheepskin slipper business) and the Kendal industry dates from 1842. The second half of the

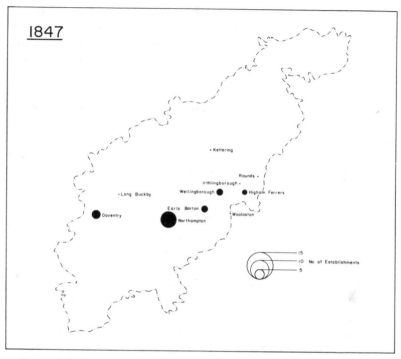

Figure 24. Boot and shoe manufacturing establishments in Northamptonshire, 1847. (Redrawn from Mounfield, P.R. 'The footwear industry of the East Midlands: (III) Northamptonshire 1700-1911', *East Midland Geographer*, Vol. 3 (8), 1965, fig. 2, p.436.)

century, the period of mechanisation and the factory, witnessed the great expansion of the industry in Leicester and rural Northamptonshire (figures 24-27). Leicester had made boots and children's shoes for some time; expansion in the 1850s — as at Kendal — related to the reluctance of Northampton and Stafford to introduce machinery. Leicester possessed a pioneer inventor and innovator, Crick, who invented a boot-riveting machine in 1853 — the first of a series of such inventions — and alone among Leicester bootmakers he was using steam power in the early 1860s. Leicester possessed other advantages — surplus labour in its hosiery and knitwear trade and the presence of an elastic web industry at the time when elastic-sided boots were coming into fashion. By 1891 Leicester had almost twice as many workers in the industry as Northampton and firms from

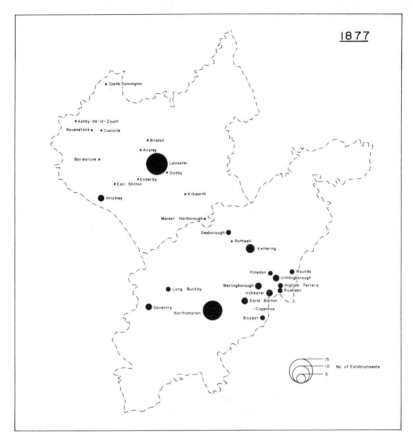

Figure 25. Boot and shoe manufacturing establishments in North-amptonshire and Leicestershire, 1877. (Redrawn from same sources as figure 24, and Mounfield, P.R., 'The footwear industry of the East Midlands: (IV) Leicesershire to 1911', *East Midland Geographer*, Vol. 4 (1), 1966, fig. 2, p.12)

elsewhere were setting up depots and branches in the county. Rural Northamptonshire offered different advantages: the whole outwork tradition of the industry favoured dispersal, and dispersed through the county was a pool of unemployed or underemployed labour, in part from a dying wool trade. This cheap labour was eminently suitable for the new machine boot business and it had provided the base for some development of the industry in the first half of the century. Undoubtedly the railway built through the Ise valley in 1857 facilitated its

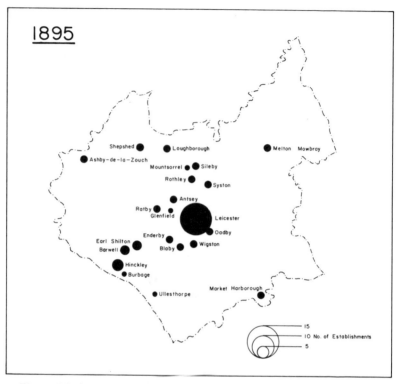

Figure 26. Boot and shoe manufacturing establishments in Leicestershire, 1895. (Redrawn from Leicestershire source for figure 25).

growth as a centre of the industry, the rapid economic (and demographic) transformation of 11 small centres (two of them old markets) into a boot and shoe manufactory set apart from the local rural economy. Absence of coal may have been a further advantage to the boot and shoe manufacturer as other industries were not attracted to the area to compete for its labour. The middle decades of the century were certainly a boom period — Northamptonshire's boot and shoe manufacturers (bespoke excepted) numbered 97 in 1847, 220 only 30 years later. But the factory system was still in the future and the industry remained largely domestic — even in northern cities, Leeds for example — and hand- or foot-powered until after 1880. The creation of the modern factory industry relates very largely to the impact of American competition and

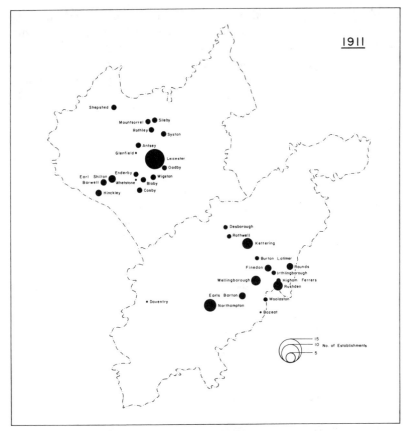

Figure 27. Boot and shoe factories in Northamptonshire and Leicestershire, 1911. (Redrawn from same sources as figures 24 and 25.)

technology by means of the American-owned British United Shoe Machinery Company of 1899.

Spatial differentiation, as complex as in wool or cotton, took two forms. Different processes were carried out in separate plants, presupposing that movement of half-made goods from plant to plant — often in fact a short journey within the one town or village — was economically possible. More significantly, different areas worked for different sections of what the railways had made a single national (and substantial export) market. Stafford made the best women's, Northampton the best men's, boots and shoes, while Leicestershire and Northampton-shire, the newcomers, made the cheaper grades. In general larger centres made higher quality goods. Bristol specialised in work boots, Rossendale in slippers, and, at an even more specialised level, Raunds had been making army boots since the Napoleonic War. As a result the bulk of the population were more cheaply and comfortably[21] shod in 1900 than in 1800; mechanisation and specialisation had benefited customer, craftsman and capitalist.

Gloving was an even more tenaciously conservative and domestic trade than boot and shoe making. London, Worcester and Yeovil were its ancient centres, the first two concerned more with fancy gloves, the last with heavier goods. In the provinces the industry was — and is — very largely domestic, but as with boot and shoe manufacture cutting was often central-ised (plate 17). Unfortunately the industry was one of fashion, more so and from an earlier date than boots and shoes, liable to instant changes and fluctuations after such events as Huskisson's removal of the prohibition of French imports in 1830, or for no apparent cause at all. Fashion was to the glover what the state of, say, the Australian economy or North American tariffs, to cite two important export markets, was to the bootmaker.

KNITWEAR AND HOSIERY

Parallels between the knitwear industry and the boot and shoe trade in the nineteenth century are at once apparent. Both were tenaciously domestic, both were carried on — and to some extent overlapped — in the East Midlands. It seems likely that in each case localisation reflected broadly similar circumstances, the availability of labour in a well populated rural area with a rather moribund domestic textile tradition and no strongly competing growth industry. However the hosiery and knitwear trade had a longer history of localisation than boot and shoe making, it was rather more subject to whims of fashion[22] and also to the reality of competition from (or at least substitution by) garments made at home by the housewife and her daughters, a commonplace even in the 1970s.

The industry's geographical localisation owed something to William Lee's invention of the stocking frame at Calverton, near

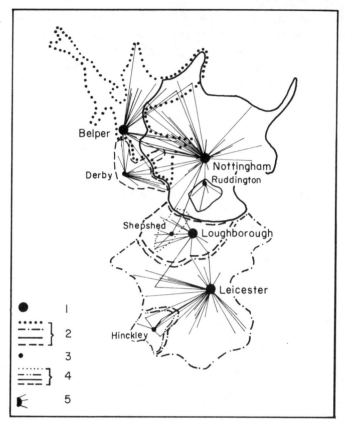

Figure 28. The domestic system in the East Midlands hosiery trade, 1844: 1, principal putting-out centres; 2, spheres of influence of principal centres; 3, secondary putting-out centres; 4, spheres of influence of secondary centres; 5, places for which there is evidence of centre worked for. (Redrawn from Smith, D.M., 'The British hosiery industry at the middle of the nineteenth century', *Institute of British Geographers : Transactions and Papers*, vol. 32, 1963, fig. 4.)

Nottingham, in 1589. By the 1840s 90 per cent of the industry's machines, providing 100,000 jobs, were in Leicestershire, Nottinghamshire or Derbyshire. These were the hand-machines of a domestic industry (plate 18) dispersed within defined areas around central warehouses. Beyond a fixed radius from these depots the quest for cheap labour became uneconomic. The industry remained thus organised until about 1850:

'it was not only that there were special technical difficulties in applying power to knitting machinery. With a superabundance of cheap labour available, employers had no incentive.'[23] Or to quote another historian of the mid-nineteenth century: 'the over-riding impression was of almost complete stagnation . . . not the least important reason for this was the existence of a well-established system of putting out'.[24] (figure 28). This situation had sad social consequences — framework knitters were even more of a byword for poverty than handloom weavers: 'the industry had entered into a transitional stage between the domestic and factory systems, and it was precisely in the trades which had arrived at this position in the first decades of the nineteenth century that the worst abuses and most oppressive conditions could be found'.[25] The industry had its secondary centres, Tewkesbury, Hawick, Dumfries, and its offshoots, most notably Nottingham lace, and from 1816 Tiverton lace when the Luddites forced Heathcoat to leave Nottingham. The main hosiery and knitwear centres were Nottingham and Leicester, followed by Hinckley, Mansfield, and Sutton-in-Ashfield, but it was above all an industry of village workers serving and serviced by warehouses in these towns.

Steam came to the industry first at Loughborough in 1839, to Nottingham in 1851, and not until the mid-sixties could high class goods be factory made. Thus in 1860 there were only somewhere between 3,000 and 4,000 factory workers in Nottingham as against 50,000 domestic; in 1862 only some three per cent of the industry's labour force came under the Factory Acts. In these circumstances the move to factories (plates 18 and 19) reflected not sudden and overwhelming technical change but legislation hostile to domestic manufacture, Frame Rent abolition (1874),[26] the Workshop Acts (1867-76), compulsory education, and the wishes of unions and employers (if not of all work people). Parallels with the boot and shoe industry are evident. The factory came first to the larger towns, the old distributive centres — Nottingham (plate 28) and Leicester which had only 22 per cent of the industry's plant in 1884 had 75 per cent 20 years later — some indication, perhaps an exaggerated one, of the triumph of the urban industry in mid-century. The process was one of some substitution of capital for labour,[27] but also of higher wages, in places

1. A Lancashire colliery, c. 1800. The setting is rural but smoky; attention is focused on pumping, weighing, and on moving coal by cart, pack donkey, and even wheelbarrow.

2. The country around Manchester, c. 1800. Manchester and to a lesser extent Oldham and Ashton-under-Line are already considerable towns; but despite conspicuous ribbon development along main roads there remains much open country.

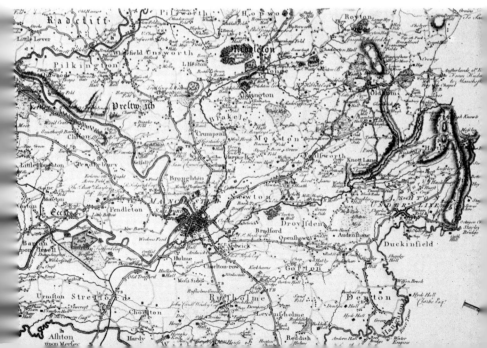

3. The country around Blackpool, *c.* 1800. A rural England of both nuclear villages (e.g. Thistleton) and dispersed hamlets and farms (e.g. east of Kirkham) untouched by industrialisation. Note the incipient Blackpool, the much older Lytham, and the limited extent of coastal settlement.

4. The Red Lion Street area of Narrow Marsh, central Nottingham, prior to demolition in 1919. Note the mixture of industry and housing. Demolition (or decay) has revealed the cross-section of a 'back-to-back' terrace; at right angles to it runs the 'blind back' of a 'not-through' terrace.

THE NEW HOUSE.

Paterfamilias (with his belongings) returned last night from the Sea-side to his new home in the Suburbs. He has slept on his own spring-bed and breakfasted comfortably, and is beginning to forget the misery of the last four weeks. The children are out. The October sun is shining brightly. A faint fragrance pervades the house, which (he says) reminds him purely of days gone by. He strolls into his garden. The young Virginia creeper is turning lovely red ; the kitten has grown into a cat, and a lily has actually burst into blossom from a bulb of his own planting. In the fulness of his heart, he throws himself into a garden chair, takes out his pipe, and begins to warble " *Home ! sweet Home !* " when—O horror ! . . . He suddenly descries a series of ominous cracks running up the back of his " *newly-built substantial semi-detached suburban residence* "—and the partner of his joys rushes out to tell him that " that subtle aroma, so poetically suggestive of the past, proceeds from—*THE DRAINS !* "

5. Mr Punch's comment on 19th-century building standards ; note the attention paid to both the structure itself and to the drains. Houses in this style survive in large numbers in the inner suburbs of many English towns and cities.

6. The blind back wall of 'not through ' houses, Lower Acreman Street, Sherborne. Compare plate 4. These stone-built cottages are probably early nineteenth-century, but note brick chimneys and later addition of the odd window.

7. Choppington Street, Newcastle upon Tyne. Built 1876-7 and photographed 1965; subsequently demolished. Certainly not a mean street with its tiny front gardens and stone doorways and windows. Note the survival of a cobbled road surface.

8. The blast furnaces at Summerlea, Monkland, Lanarkshire, in the late 1870s: the classic Scottish iron and steel industry in its prime, served by canal as well as railway.

9. Oldham from Glodwick *c.* 1831. Numerous mills and chimneys are in evidence; the new church – a sign of the wealth generated by the cotton industry – is conspicuous on the skyline, but the setting remains rural.

10. Oldham from Glodwick *c.* 1870. A closer and murkier view than plate 9 – a transformation from rural to urban. Several factory chimneys can be identified in both plates; note too the conspicuous presence of mines among mills.

11. (*above*) Huddersfield *c.* 1830. A small town in a rural setting but note the already numerous mill chimneys, bleaching grounds (?) (right middle distance), and mills outside the town (often set in a cluster of houses, e.g. left foreground) and some distance from it.

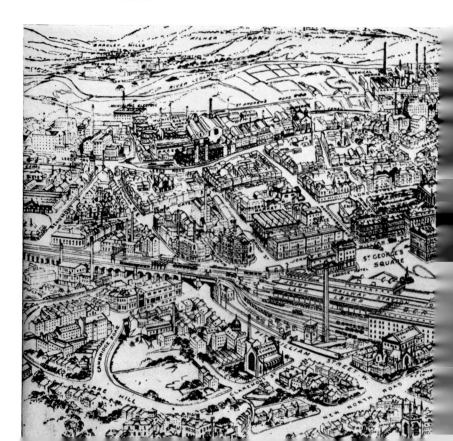

12. (*below*) Huddersfield in 1900. Note the growth of the town and its satellites, the numerous churches and schools as well as mills. The railways have conspicuously occupied the open space prominent in the foreground of the 1830 view (plate 11) but provision has been made for a park and there is some evidence of suburban sprawl.

13. St Rollox Chemical Works, Glasgow, *c.* 1878. The very tall chimneys (known locally as 'Tennant's stalks') were typical of the Leblanc process, the rather impermanent looking buildings of most branches of nineteenth-century chemical industry.

14. Ardeer explosive works, Ayrshire, in the early 1870s, shortly after their establishment. Note dispersal among and inside dunes for safety and the conspicuous hill-top lookout. The works eventually became part of ICI.

15. Vernon's new flour mills, Birkenhead Dock. Built in 1899 this mill is a classic example of the large dockside roller mill of the late nineteenth century, dependent on imported supplies and rail distribution.

16. West Mill, Sherborne, *c.* 1900. The opposite end of the spectrum from plate 15. A water-powered mill in a rural area milling local supplies for local needs. As was often the case the mill, now ruinous, is located a short distance from the town.

17. A glove-cutting room in Yeovil *c.* 1898. As in the boot and shoe trade cutting was early centralised and its practitioners were among the most skilled and most highly paid employees. Note the minimal machinery, the use of hand tools.

18. Framework knitters' cottages, Currant Street, Nottingham; built *c.* 1800, photographed *c.* 1919. The well-lit workrooms comprising the upper storeys (and in this case attics) are characteristic of domestic textile manufacture; note also cellars and the effect of the height of the buildings in shutting out sunlight.

PREMISES OF MESSRS. HINE, MUNDELLA, AND CO.

19. The hosiery factory of Hine, Mundella and Co., Station Street, Nottingham, 1856. The first of the town's hosiery factories, it was opened in 1851. Note sheep and cattle in the street and the paucity of vehicular traffic; the location of the new premises in Station Street is scarcely coincidental.

20. S.S. *Elderslie* berthed at Oamaru, New Zealand. Built by Palmers of Jarrow in 1884 this steamer was the first built specifically for the New Zealand frozen meat trade. Oamaru was the port for the area which pioneered the trade. Thus the picture epitomises British maritime and shipbuilding supremacy and dependence on imported food.

21.   Channel Island steamers at Weymouth *c.* 1880. At this date the service was somewhat run-down and the paddle steamers, some 40 years old, do not represent the best contemporary packet steamers. Note numerous sailing vessels astern of steamers.

22.   London General Omnibus Company Stables, Hackney 1901: the bus depot of the period, horses requiring space, labour and food.

23. Hayboats on the Thames *c.* 1872. Provisioning London's horses was a very substantial problem and perhaps a limit to city growth.

POST OFFICE REGULATIONS.

ON AND AFTER THE 10th JANUARY, a Letter not exceeding HALF AN OUNCE IN WEIGHT, may be sent from any part of the United Kingdom, to any other part, for ONE PENNY, if paid when posted, or for TWO PENCE if paid when delivered.

THE SCALE OF RATES,

If paid when posted, is as follows, for all Letters, whether sent by the General or by any Local Post,

Not exceeding ½ Ounce	**One Penny.**
Exceeding ½ Ounce, but not exceeding 1 Ounce	**Twopence.**
Ditto 1 Ounce ... . 2 Ounces	**Fourpence.**
Ditto 2 Ounces .... 3 Ounces	**Sixpence.**

and so on; an additional Two-pence for every additional Ounce. With but few exceptions, the WEIGHT is limited to Sixteen Ounces.

If not paid when posted, double the above Rates are charged on Inland Letters.

COLONIAL LETTERS.

If sent by Packet Twelve Times, if by Private Ship Eight Times, the above Rates.

FOREIGN LETTERS.

The Packet Rates which vary, will be seen at the Post Office. The Ship Rates are the same as the Ship Rates for Colonial Letters.

As regards Foreign and Colonial Letters, there is no limitation as to weight. All sent outwards, with a few exceptions, which may be learnt at the Post Office, must be paid when posted as heretofore.

Letters intended to go by Private Ship must be marked "*Ship Letter.*"

Some arrangements of minor importance, which are omitted in this Notice, may be seen in that placarded at the Post Office.

No Articles should be transmitted by Post which are liable to *injury* by being stamped, or by being crushed in the Bags.

It is particularly requested that all Letters may be *fully* and *legibly* addressed, and *posted as early* as convenient.

January 7th, 1840.

By Authority :—J. Hartnell. London.

24. The 'penny post' regulation of 1840. Note the geographical emphasis and transformation, 'from any part of the United Kingdom, to any other part', the very high foreign rates, and the perennial appeal for legibility and correct address.

25. An early Victorian milk shop: cows are kept on the premises (hay in the basement) and customers supplied with milk, eggs, cheese and butter.

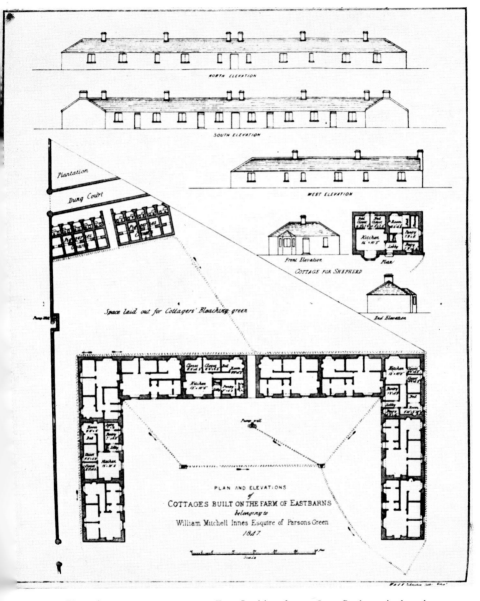

NORTH ELEVATION

SOUTH ELEVATION

WEST ELEVATION

Plantation

Dung Court

Space laid out for Cottagers' Bleaching green

Front Elevation

COTTAGE FOR SHEPHERD

Plan

Kitchen

End Elevation

Kitchen

Pump well

PLAN AND ELEVATIONS
of
COTTAGES BUILT ON THE FARM OF EASTBARNS
belonging to
William Mitchell Innes Esquire of Parsons Green
1847

Scale

26. Plans for new cottages on an East Lothian farm 1847. Such agricultural 'barracks' can still be seen in this area of traditionally expert farming. The cost of each cottage was about £110; note very small size (about 600 sq. ft.), absence of gardens (but provision of piggery) and the superior, detached shepherd's cottage.

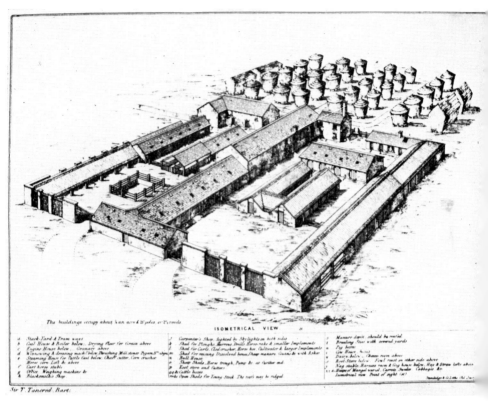

The buildings occupy about ½ an acre & 2½ poles or 2½ reeds

ISOMETRICAL VIEW

a Stack Yard & Tram ways
b Coal House & Boiler below . Drying Floor for Grain above
c Engine House below . Granary above
d Winnowing & dressing machine below Thrashing Mill stones Pigeon H^{se} above
e Steaming House for Cattle food below. Chaff cutter, Corn crusher
f Horse corn Loft &c above
f Cart horse stable
g Office. Weighing machine &c
h Blacksmiths Shop

i Carpenter's Shop, lighted by Skylights on both sides
k Shed for Ploughs. Harrows Drills Horse rake & smaller Implements
l Shed for Carts, Clod crusher. Horse hoe Cultivator & Larger Implements
m Shed for mixing Dissolved bones Sheep manure Guano &c with Ashes
n Bull House
o Sheep Sheds Horse trough, Pump &c at further end
p Root store and Cutter
q & r Cattle houses
r & s Open Sheds for Young Stock. The roofs may be ridged

s Manure depôt should be roofed
t Breeding Sow with covered yards
u Pig barn
v Cow House &c &c
w Dairy below . Cheese room above
x Root-Store below. Fowl roost on other side above
y Nag stable. Harness room & Gig house below. Hay & Straw lofts above
z &c House of Mangel wurzel. Carrots. Swedes. Cabbages &c

Isometrical view Board of Right ½

Sir T. Tancred Bart.

27. Prize-winning farm layout of 1850. Note the extensive buildings, the large rickyard, and the engine-house.

28. Smallholder's cottage at Rew, Dorchester, built *c.* 1890 on an 8-acre holding. The pioneer fringe of the depression period was, to some politicians at least, a panacea. This corrugated iron shack suggests another view.

with established transport links to markets and now ready access to coal. However the last decades of the century witnessed a revival of the traditional geography, the spread of factories into rural areas in search of cheap (often non-union) labour, and away from such competitors in the labour market as lace in west Nottinghamshire, the boot and shoe trade in Leicestershire, and Boot, Player and Raleigh in Nottingham. The movement did not take the form of migration to the coalfields since coal was widely available and not very important. Nottingham and Leicester's share of the industry fell from 62 per cent in 1881 to 42 per cent in 1899, but dispersal of the industry was largely contained within its traditional limits. In fact, as Smith has pointed out, there is a remarkable correlation between the size of mid-century domestic manufacture and late nineteenth-century factory industry throughout the northeast Midlands. Regional pre-eminence increased to the extent that this area provided 95 per cent of all hosiery and knitwear employment by the 1890s. Local specialisation existed, but less strongly than in similar industries. Derby made silk hose, Nottinghamshire made cotton hose (having been engaged in cotton manufacture in the first phase of the Industrial Revolution) and lace; Leicestershire made worsted hose and woollen knitwear. Like its peers the industry had to face problems in export markets, notably tariffs and competition; characteristically wool fared better than cotton here. The bureaucrat played his part in sustaining hand-frame industry, according to one writer 'because the War Office had an antiquated specification for military pants'.[28]

SOME CONCLUSIONS

It would be possible to go on to discuss the industrial geography of nineteenth-century Britain at great length. It seems debatable that this would further facilitate generalisation, be it tentative, verbal (and thus unfashionable), confident or numerical. If a first generalisation is to describe nineteenth-century Britain as the age of coal — an almost self-evident statement — what was coal's locational impact? Certainly the iron and steel industry was drawn to the coalfields, in search of ore as well as coal, and cotton and wool were lucky enough to be situated on secondary and easily worked coalfields. The technology of these two textile trades had for the most part reached a fuel-demanding stage in the first half of the century, hence the fact that they thrived on the coalfields and languished elsewhere, although other circumstances were also involved. But it should also be pointed out that the textile trade's propensity to migrate to coal, to follow the miner eastwards in Yorkshire for example, or to venture more widely, was negligible. Other industries found the coalfields equally unattractive having not yet reached the steam power stage — leather and hosiery for example. Even the chemical industry, a considerable coal user, was not tied to the coalfields. Coalmining areas were, after all, in many cases remote, paid high wages to their workers and were equipped by mid-century to move coal to the manufacturer cheaply and reliably. He proved as reluctant to move to coal as did established coalfield industries — notably iron — to leave them.

In such conditions, once the railways could move coal almost everywhere, other factors affected industrial location. Some sought out raw materials or their port of entry — iron and steel in Cleveland, Cumberland and South Wales, paper around London (also a market), flour milling at Liverpool — and settled there. Others kept to a regional pattern set up long ago, perhaps by a forgotten entrepreneur or inventor and his successors. They had reached only a hand tool stage in the first half of the century and by the time they became coal users — footwear and hosiery for example — it was easier for the coal to come to them than for them to move. A pool of cheap rural labour was often to their advantage and played a part in their late nineteenth-century geography, as it had at an earlier date for cotton and wool. Public pressure was by no means insignificant, in the chemical trades for example, and in the guise of specialised markets and tastes it affected the geography of both paper-making and brewing. The importance of inter-industry linkages is evident, as on Tyneside, and their significance within industries increased as the subdivision of processes was extended and specialised common commercial and technical services came into use; hence the propensity for local 'swarming'.

The coal-fired steam locomotive had served to carry coal to the customer rather than customer to coal, save in those instances where the customer ante-dated the means of communication. Timing of technological change — of the application of power and of the direct use of coal — is thus all-important. Broadly speaking if it occurred before mid-century the industry located on the coalfields, if after mid-century there was a high probability, in old-established industries in particular, that the coal would be brought to existing sites or their vicinity. 'Changes in the geographical distribution of industry since 1850 have not been general . . . the major interest of the years 1850-1913 with regard to most industries is of trends in the balance of output as between different regional centres and of changes in the detailed distribution of industries within regions already roughly defined by the middle of the nineteenth century'.[29] The preceding century or so had been quite exceptional in the propensity of industry to move and adjust its locations, but after 1850 there was a return to the more usual inertia and immobility.[30]

NOTES

1 von Liebig, J., *Familiar Letters on Chemistry,* London, 1843, p.30. This book went through four editions in English by 1859, perhaps an indication that science was neither so unpopular nor so neglected in nineteenth-century Britain as has sometimes been suggested.

2 This remains the case, witness any modern textbook of chemistry.

3 Barilla, containing about 25% alkali, was obtained by burning a Mediterranean plant. The trade was closely associated with Alicante and thus very subject to interruption during the several eighteenth-century wars with Spain. Kelp was made by burning sea weed and was one of the staple industries of the Scottish Highlands and Islands. See Clow, A. and N.L., *The Chemical Revolution,* London, 1952, pp.65-90.

4 Charles Tennant, a Scottish linen bleacher — at the time a key local industry — patented bleaching powder in 1798 and set up St Rollox in 1799 for its manufacture. The works soon outgrew the needs or ends of linen, itself a contracting industry.

5 'Tennant's Stalk' at St Rollox (1842) was 420 feet high. In

general the object of tall chimneys was not only dispersal, which up to a point could increase damage, but to make more difficult the tracing of the offender.

6 Proceedings of the Town Council of Newcastle upon Tyne, 9 January 1839, p.19. Quoted by Campbell, W.A., *The Chemical Industry,* London, 1971, p.36.

7 *Daily News,* April, 1888.

8 Quoted from the patent itself by Campbell, W.A., op.cit., pp.75-6.

9 See Chapter 3, note 13. Gilchrist Thomas went so far as to assert that phosphorus would one day be the main product of his process, and threatened to sell out his interest in the North Eastern Steel Company to prevent it making a long-term, low-price contract for disposal of basic slag in 1884.

10 Rags were also used as a fertiliser and became the raw material of the shoddy trade during the first half of the nineteenth century. The concept of recycling is no twentieth-century novelty.

11 Coleman, D.C., *The British Paper Industry 1495-1860,* Oxford, 1958, p.146.

12 Beer is rarely now sold as porter, but porter is much the same as the still popular stout.

13 Even as far as India, hence the term India Pale Ale (I.P.A.).

14 The geographical basis of this advantage was the hardness — especially the gypsum content — and purity of the water supply.

15 Mathias, P., *The Brewing Industry in England 1700-1830,* Cambridge, 1959, p.xxvii.

16 Scarcely a station in Britain has not a hotel, and the course of former railways — or even merely planned lines — is evidenced in public house names, witness the 'Silent Whistle' at Evercreech on the old Somerset and Dorset Line, the 'Railway Dock Hotel' at Weymouth on the proposed, but never executed, line to the new dock.

17 To say nothing of the temperance and abstinence campaigners; the geography of alcohol as a social problem and responses to it in the nineteenth century deserves investigation.

18 In the Middle Ages the lord's mill commonly enjoyed a valuable monopoly and vestiges of this persisted.

19 He himself usually asserts that it is particularly healthy, a confidence shared not only proverbially by the farmer, but — more remarkably — by the nineteenth-century alkali manufacturer!

20 Muscott, B.B., 'Leather', in volume 2 (1906) of the *Victoria History of the County of Northampton,* p.317.

21 Bespoke boots and shoes excepted, all evidence suggests that the average boot of the pre-machine phase was poorly fitting, uncomfortable, and at worst damaging. The distinction of left from right is a late nineteenth-century phenomenon.

22 Perhaps most notable in the nineteenth century is the substitution of trousers for breeches.

23 Patterson, A. Temple, *Radical Leicester,* Leicester, 1954, p.381.

24 Head, P., 'Putting out in the Leicester hosiery industry in the middle of the nineteenth century', *Transactions of the Leicestershire Archaeological and Historical Society,* vol. 37, 1961-2, p.56.

25 Patterson, p.62.

26 Frame rent abolition outlawed the system whereby the knitter hired his machine (frame) from the master hosier, or sometimes from a middleman, to whom also he sold his finished work. Frame renting was a conservative force, favoured by manufacturers, opposed by trades unions; it appears to have been losing both economic and technical advantage even before 1874.

27 Ironically just as such staples as coal and cotton had begun to do the reverse.

28 Clapham, J.H., *An Economic History of Modern Britain: Free Trade and Steel 1850-1886,* Cambridge, 1932, quoting *Royal Commission on Labour,* 1892, Question 13358.

29 Smith, W., *An Historical Introduction to the Economic Geography of Great Britain,* London, 1968, p.161.

30 Rawstron, E.M., 'Some aspects of the location of hosiery and lace manufacture in Great Britain', *East Midland Geographer,* vol. 9, 1958, pp.16-28, ends (pp.26-8) with a useful summary of the locational forces acting on British industry as a whole in the nineteenth century.

FURTHER READING

1 CHEMICALS

Campbell, W.A., *The Chemical Industry,* London, 1971.
Campbell, W.A., *A Century of Chemistry on Tyneside 1868-1968,* Newcastle upon Tyne, 1968.
Clow, A., 'Vitriol and the Industrial Revolution', *Economic History Review,* vol. 15, 1945, pp.44-55.
Clow, A. and N.L., *The Chemical Revolution,* London, 1952.
Haber, L.F., *The Chemical Industry during the Nineteenth Century,* Oxford (2nd edition), 1969.
Hardie, D.W.F., *A History of the Chemical Industry in Widnes,* London, 1950.
Hardie, D.W.F. and Pratt, D., *A History of the Modern British Chemical Industry,* Oxford, 1966.
MacLeod, R.M., 'The Alkali Acts Administration 1863-84', *Victorian Studies,* vol. 9, 1965, pp.85-112.
Taylor, F. Sherwood, *A History of Industrial Chemistry,* London, 1957.
Wallwork, K., 'The mid-Cheshire salt industry', *Geography,* vol. 44, 1959, pp.171-86.

2 PAPER

Coleman, D.C., *The British Paper Industry 1495-1860,* Oxford, 1958.
Lewis, P.W., 'Changing factors of location in the paper-making industry as illustrated by the Maidstone area', *Geography,* vol. 52, 1967, pp.280-93.
Parris, H., 'Adaptation to technical change in the paper-making industry: the paper mill at Richmond, Yorkshire, 1823-46', *Yorkshire Bulletin,* vol. 12, 1960, pp.84-9.
Shorter, A.H., *Paper making in the British Isles: An Historical and Geographical Study,* Newton Abbot, 1971.

3 BREWING

Burnet, J., *Plenty and Want: A Social History of Diet in England from 1815 to the Present Day,* London, 1966 (also for flour-milling).
Mathias, P., *The Brewing Industry in England 1700-1830,* Cambridge, 1959.

Mathias, P., 'Industrial revolution in brewing', *Explorations in Entrepreneurial History,* vol. 5, 1953, pp.208-24.

Monckton, H.A., *A History of English Ale and Beer,* London, 1966.

Sigsworth, E.M., *The brewing trade during the industrial revolution: the case of Yorkshire,* York (Borthwick Papers No. 31), 1967.

Vaizey, J., *The Brewing Industry 1886-1951,* London, 1960.

4   FLOUR MILLING

Bennett, R., and Elton, J., *A History of Corn Milling,* London, 1898-1904.

5   LEATHER, FOOTWEAR, GLOVES

Church, R.A., 'The British leather industry and foreign competition 1870-1914', *Economic History Review* (2nd series), vol. 24, 1971, pp.543-68.

Church, R.A., 'The effect of the American export invasion on the British boot and shoe industry 1885-1914', *Journal of Economic History,* vol. 28, 1968, pp.223-54.

Fox, A., *A History of the National Union of Boot and Shoe Operatives 1874-1957,* Oxford, 1958.

Morley, C.D., 'Population of Northampton and the Ise Valley 1801-1951', *East Midland Geographer,* vol. 11, 1959, pp.20-29 (also hosiery and knitwear).

Mounfield, P.R., 'The footwear industry of the East Midlands', *East Midland Geographer,* vols 3 and 4, 1964-6, pp.293-306, 394-413, 434-53 and 8-23.

Patterson, A. Temple., *Radical Leicester,* Leicester, 1954.

Rimmer, W.G., 'The Leeds leather industry in the nineteenth century', *Thoresby Society Publications,* vol. 46, 1960, pp.119-64.

Weekly, I.G., 'Industry in the small country towns of Lincolnshire, Northamptonshire and Rutland', *East Midland Geographer,* vol. 7, 1957, pp.21-30.

6   HOSIERY AND KNITWEAR

Church, R.A., *Economic and Social Change in a Midland Town: Victorian Nottingham, 1815-1900,* London, 1966.

Head, P., 'Putting out in the Leicester hosiery industry in the middle of the nineteenth century', *Transactions of the*

Leicestershire Archaeological and Historical Society, vol. 37, 1961-2, pp.44-59.

Rawstron, E.M., 'Some aspects of the location of hosiery and lace manufacture in Great Britain', *East Midland Geographer,* vol. 9, 1958, pp.16-28.

Smith, D.M., 'The British hosiery industry at the middle of the nineteenth century: an historical study in economic geography', *Institute of British Geographers : Transactions,* vol. 32, 1963, pp.125-42.

Smith, D.M., 'The location of the British hosiery industry since the late nineteenth century', *East Midland Geographer,* vol. 5, 1970, pp.71-9.

Wells, F.A., *The British Hosiery and Knitwear Industry: Its History and Organisation,* Newton Abbot (revised edition), 1972.

6 Movement and Mobility: The Conquest of Distance

The nineteenth century was a century of easier movement, of the creation of the railway and the steamer and of their colossal impact on the economy and society. This impact is a major theme of most socio-economically oriented studies of nineteenth-century Britain and the Railway Age has even generated at least one history of the period organised around this topic.[1] More characteristically studies of the period briefly discuss the demise of turnpike and canal and then plunge into a prolonged discussion of the glories of the railway; the steamer, perhaps even the motor car, provides a postcript. This approach, organising the topic of transport in terms of medium, inevitably and rightly gives pride of place to the railway, even in balanced and imaginative studies which have not succumbed to the lure of steam. It is to be doubted however whether this is to put the railway into an apt perspective; railways, like every other means of communication, existed neither in their own right nor to complete a centralised plan — nor even for the delight of later generations — but to facilitate the movement of goods and people either for the profit of promoter and proprietor, or at the behest (and subsidy) of the state or a benefactor-philanthropist. The railways of nineteenth-century Britain thus resemble the airlines of the last quarter of the twentieth — they are there, conspicuous and even a matter for intermittent public debate. Evidently they have a considerable impact on economy and society since they are a big business in their own right, but the economy and society had showed themselves capable of advance before they were created, and only a small part of the population is a direct user of their services. Moreover railway and aeroplane depend on other means of transport, the motor vehicle or, in the nineteenth century, the horse, without which they are stranded whales or lame ducks. For most people of the nineteenth century walking was the normal means of movement — the car is becoming a close twentieth-century analogy — and yet the pedestrian rarely enters scholarly discussion of the topic or the period; likewise the horse, although Thompson has begun to redress this omission[2], real and counterfactual. Moreover nineteenth-century Britain was provided with a variety of other means of communication — the telegraph, a much improved postal service, new-style newspapers, and by the end of the century near universal literacy. These new means of spreading ideas and information deserve discussion alongside more visible and conspicuous methods. The framework of this chapter is not, then, how it moved (or was moved), but what moved, and how far, and where? Geographers have often employed this approach, studies of the 'journey to work' for example, and it appears equally appropriate for areas which they have neglected such as information and finance; hopefully it will also prove applicable to coal, corn and commuters. But firstly the distinction between movement inland and overseas must be made.

OVERSEAS

There was only one way of leaving Britain during the nineteenth century — by sea. This might be the 20 or so miles to Calais or the 12,000 to the Antipodes, but in either case there was no alternative to a sea voyage — no airports, no hovercraft, and only the idea of a Channel Tunnel.[3] Nevertheless the nineteenth century witnessed the transformation of every aspect of this maritime traffic; Brittania ruled the waves, commercially as well as militarily, from a position of much loftier and lonelier pre-eminence at the end of the century than at the beginning. By 1914 one-third of the world's merchant shipping — and one half of launchings — were British. Sail had yielded to steam as the steamer had progressed from a primitive and pioneering toy to a peak of near perfection. There is a strong case for regarding the great passenger, or even cargo, liner of the 1890s as the apogee of nineteenth-century technical and organisational attainment. Not only the ships but their management and operations had been transformed, by their owners and operators, by government intervention, by telegraphy.

Britain attained an unquestioned, albeit not unchallenged, maritime supremacy only in the latter half of the century, and as much by accident as by design. It was not only a question of British economic development being dependent upon and the generator of more traffic, for the carrying trade for third parties was a major part of Britain's maritime activity. Nor was it merely the abundance of coal and iron which allowed Britain to take the lead in the technical revolution in ship construction. Britain's principal maritime rival in the early nineteenth century, the U.S.A., suffered greatly from the Civil War, its timing particularly unfortunate from the maritime point of view. The repeal of the protective Navigation Acts in 1849 and 1854 although resisted by British shipowners proved to be to their benefit and demonstrated that most foreign owners were unable to compete in most trades.

Commercial pre-eminence emerged in the two decades 1850-1870; the technical transformation was protracted. If *Charlotte Dundas* (1802) was the first steamer and *Comet* (1812) the first commercial steamer, only about 70 years later did the nominal carrying capacity of British steam exceed that of sail. As late as 1900 it was no problem to obtain a passage to Australia by sail and many of the minor ports of Britain were still concerned largely with sailing vessels. Until the compound steam engine was developed in the 1860s the commercial possibilities of the steam engine were limited by high fuel consumption — which raised costs and limited cargo space — and a limited infrastructure of coaling stations. Steamers were effectively limited to short routes and/or high value traffic, commonly combined in passenger routes. These were the steamer's first area of success so that by 1825 so many were competing for Belfast-Glasgow passengers that the first class fare was 2s (10p), the deck passage free.[4] Customers were ready to pay for the speed and regularity which steam alone, and from early in its history, could provide. On longer routes, the North Atlantic or via the Mediterranean or to India, suitable steamships were slower to develop and a government mail subsidy was essential for viability. On this basis private enterprise, the Pensinular and Oriental (P.&O.) for example, could oust the old East Indiamen and the Admiralty Mail service. The mails also mattered for short routes such as the Channel Islands.[5] By 1860 mail subsidies were costing the government a million pounds a year, a modest price however for so much improved a service. Long haul bulk cargoes remained the realm of sail until the end of the century and some of these trades, newly developed, were ideal for the large sailing vessel. Australian wool for example came from a distant continent by a route remote from bunkering stations and favourable to sail because of the strong westerly winds of the Southern Hemisphere. Even the first cargoes of frozen mutton from New Zealand in 1881 came under sail, a decade and a half after Holt had introduced the first economical long-range cargo steamers in 1865. He operated iron-built, compound-engined, screw-propelled steamers in the rich China trade, where the Suez Canal was to add to steam's advantages; he soon had his successful imitators. As steamers grew bigger so they needed proportionately less power and were cheaper to run; as the steamer became ubiquitous so did the market for British steam coal. Freight rates fell markedly — it had cost £6 to ship a ton of cotton to Shanghai in 1866, £2 in 1913. This was one element in the possibility and actuality of a greater dependence on world trade — 'international trade . . . ceased to be an affair of luxuries and became instead a constant daily procession of indispensable necessities'[6] — and a great increase in tonnage. British ports handled 18.5 million tons of shipping in 1855, 139 million tons in 1912.

The transformation was organisational as well as technological and geographical. The passenger liner, the tramp, and the shipping company are nineteenth-century creations and only the cargo liner (plate 20) can be regarded as a close relative of an early nineteenth-century pattern of operations, the East Indianman or Newfoundland trader for example, working as nearly to a fixed schedule as the elements allowed. Regularity depended on steam, and passenger liners also needed a sure flow of traffic generated on the one hand by new prosperity, on the other by old adversity — emigration. Thus such well known lines as Cunard (1840) and Royal Mail (1840) were set up, though their present form reflects subsequent amalgamations, each specialising in a particular area and set of routes. The tramp[7] arrives later, in the 1880s and 1890s; bulk cargoes had long been carried, but the tramp in its classical form was created by the conjunction of cheap steamers and a worldwide telegraph network. By 1914 they dominated world trade although their eventual rival, the specialist bulk carrier, had already appeared on the scene in the guise of the oil tanker. Moreover oil was starting to displace coal as a fuel. It was the tramp rather than the liner which ousted sail from its last strongholds in overseas and coastwise trade. The role of the telegraph was to give the owner continuous and worldwide commercial control over operations, so increasingly he came to be a London or Liverpool based limited company. After 1875 he was also likely, outside the North Atlantic and tramp trades, to participate in a conference, fixing rates and schedules to his own, and less certainly his customer's, advantage.

Each one of these changes, aided by the railways, acted to concentrate foreign trade more and more onto a few major ports. From an early stage these assisted the process by opening new docks and building more and better warehouses. Liverpool had six docks by 1796 and during the nineteenth century the longest interval between dock openings in the port was only 12 years. London saw a particularly intense period of activity early in the century – it had no docks in 1796, six by 1811. The lesser ports declined relatively and in many cases absolutely. Poole lost its 300-year old Newfoundland and Mediterranean trade for example; Weymouth came to concentrate on old and new Channel Island traffic (plate 21), passengers and potatoes for example, largely to the exclusion of a wider range of continental and coastwise trades. New technology, new telegraphs, new trades transformed a maritime geography of the small, the dispersed, the occasional, into a new geography of the large, the concentrated and the regular.

GOODS

The most general and diverse group of commodities – alum and antimacassars, ale and apples – presents the widest range of alternative, competing, and at times replacing, transport possibilities. As in the 1970s it also presented in the nineteenth century the largest number of special cases, exceptions and anomalies. Thus the Railway Clearing House soon found that any classification brings problems – its own initial (1842) six class (five plus special and exclusions) system had grown to a book of 129 pages by 1879 even though based on the simple

Figure 29. Canals and inland waterways of Britain c. 1820. Note that only in central England and central Scotland was there any kind of continuous system. (Redrawn from Hadfield, C.M., *The Canal Age*, Newton Abbot, 1968, fig. 3.)

idea of value. Pictures, poultry (alive) and silk (manufactured), to name but three 5th (and highest) class items of the 1852 list raise the separate problems of fragility, perishability, and pillageability.

Most early nineteenth-century railway promoters set out to solve the problem of the cost of the carriage of bulky goods.

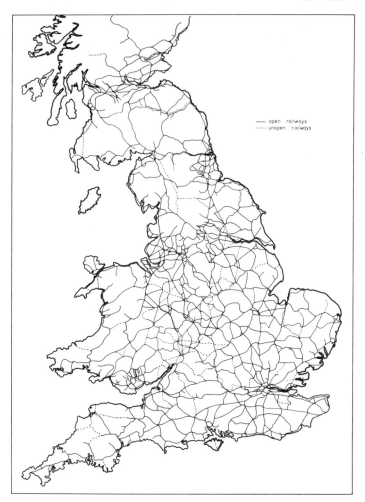

Figure 30. The railways of Britain in 1872. By this date the network was approaching its maximum extent; compare with figure 29. (Redrawn from *Report on Railway Amalgamations*, 1872.)

The railway as we know it grew out of local solutions, coalfield solutions in particular, to this problem, and from efforts to find alternatives to the coaster and canal and their limitations. These flourished in the early nineteenth century; the second canal boom was as late as the 1820s (figure 29) and the Tyne coal trade required as much shipping as the whole overseas trade. But even in the lowland zone many areas were remote from ports and, even after two construction booms, from canals. The railways penetrated every corner of Britain (figure 30), depriving coaster and canal of some, but not all of their business, and reducing waterway freight rates by about half between 1820 and 1866. Their success was neither instantaneous nor absolute, for as late as 1863 eight times as much traffic between Edinburgh/Glasgow and London went by sea as by rail;[8] railway companies had to learn the art and science of railway operation and to create such institutions as the Clearing House. Water-borne carriage, sea or canal, remained optimal for some goods over wide areas and for a wider range of goods within narrower geographical limits. Only in 1867 did more rail than sea coal come to London, and the Oxford Canal was carrying as much traffic in in the 1860s as 40 years earlier, but at one-third of the price to pay one quarter of the dividend. In whatever way goods were carried they generally began and ended their journey by horse and cart, the forgotten transport medium of the nineteenth century. Pickfords alone had 4,000 horses in the 1820s for their fast Birmingham-London boats and, moreover, the coalfield alternative to the canal system, the tramway, also used some horses, just as the whole industry depended on the horse for underground haulage. In fact, as Perkin has observed, one consequence of the railways was that 'more horse drawn vehicles than ever appeared on the roads',[9] requiring skilled labour, country-bred replacements, country-grown oats, and a great deal of space.

The railways did not take over the whole of the bulk trade but in attaining pre-eminence therein they evened out the geographical pattern of advantage and disadvantage inherent in the coaster and canal system. Their impact on the carriage of small consignments of more valuable goods — 'parcels' — was more rapid. The growth of business, of the economy as a whole, in the nineteenth century necessitated such a cheap, speedy and reliable service. The coach, the canal, the carrier's cart could not offer all of these simultaneously, and only in the cities could the pedestrian messenger offer an adequate service — as he still does in some cases. The railways were quick to see and seize the opportunity, and in the absence of competition could maintain rates high enough to pay a good profit. Sometimes they used the experience, personnel, and infrastructure of old-established firms, Pickfords for example, and they also developed their own essential organisation for an effective nationwide service, the Clearing House. This institution acted for the railways in obstructing, and preventing, the establishment of a rival for traffic of this kind, the Post Office Parcel Post, until 1883. Bulk freight and parcels did not make up the whole goods traffic: a variety of other potentially lucrative, albeit practically inconvenient, business awaited development. From the late 1860s the railways handled the greater part of London's rapidly growing milk demand, likewise — on a smaller scale — in other cities. Perishable fruit and vegetables similarly depended on the railways in many instances — only when an integrated railway and steamer service was provided via Weymouth did the Channel Island tomato trade flourish. Livestock belongs to a similar category, for the railways killed the traditional pattern of movement of lean beasts from Wales and Scotland 'on the hoof' to such markets as Horsham St Faith, and replaced it by a fatstock and dead meat trade serving weekly or daily markets. Towns such as Craven Arms grew up on this basis. The steamer could however still rival the railway for some of the live traffic, from Aberdeenshire to London for example, not because it was speedier or cheaper but because the beasts were delivered in better condition.

The railways grew out of a set of local solutions to a 'goods' problem and though their passenger business soon captured the public and entrepreneurial imagination, by 1852 goods traffic had regained the role of provider of the greater part of the revenue. The railway companies were busily purchasing, neglecting, and less often closing, the canals, reducing them to a local, feeder role; they were cutting back the sphere of influence of the now diminishing number of ports engaged in coastwise trade to a thin fringe within which the railway itself was often a feeder and distributor. The small amount of long-distance road traffic extant in 1800 was taken over and massively developed; the old economic disadvantage of an inland location had largely, but not wholly, disappeared. 'The major contribution of the railways was not so much to lower freight charges . . . as to quicken bulk transport and to extend it to areas beyond the reach of canals'.[10] Flexibility and speed as much as cheapness were the railway's advantages, but it remained dependent on the horse as a distributor and vulnerable to the horseless carriage as a competitor.

PASSENGERS

The travelling public of nineteenth-century Britain was as diverse and varied as its goods, in the purposes for which it travelled, in the length of its purse, in the time at its disposal. The century of the railway was the first in which the common man — proverbially on the Clapham omnibus[11] — might also expect to undertake an occasional long-distance excursion. The Great Exhibition of 1851 was perhaps the first, certainly the best known, but by no means the only such occasion. The journey to work was not a nineteenth-century creation, but nineteenth-century developments provided a range of alternative methods which substantially extended its geographical limits for the greater part of the population. The amalgam of alternatives is however like the iceberg; what is concealed and unseen is more remarkable than what is evident and conspicuous.

For by far the largest group throughout the century the journey to work was a walk. As early as 1836 100,000 pedestrians crossed London Bridge daily. In 1854 four times as many people walked to work in London as used any other method; a survey of trades unionists — skilled and unskilled — in South London in 1896 revealed that only one quarter ever used public transport. In some areas there was no alternative — the farm labourer walked up to four or five miles to work,[12] some country children almost as far to school — and even the workmens' trains and the trams were too costly for some of those they were intended to serve. Society was adjusted and accustomed to pedestrianism — it may even have preferred it. Jagger's clerk, Wemmick, in *Great Expectations* walked in to work each day from Walworth to Smithfield even though he could probably have afforded to use a bus; Liverpool's suburban expansion in the period 1831-1871 scarcely extends beyond walking distance from the city centre. A large number of the casually and irregularly employed had to live close to where they were likeliest to find work — the docks, the markets — but the overall impression is of a pedestrian society, adjusted to this norm, accepting its advantages, and tolerating the high urban densities it necessitated. No doubt this was one reason why the Sunday excursion was so popular. The decline of pedestrianism is primarily a twentieth-century phenomenon, the impact of the car on the affluent society, but with one major and one minor exception. From the late 1880s the bicycle came into common use, considerably extending the distance which working men could travel to work, and in cities the telephone made it possible to do without large numbers of hitherto commercially indispensable messengers.

The walker was as pre-eminent in the journey to work as the horse in the carriage of goods; for the rest – the minority – there remained several possibilities. A few possessed their own carriage and rather more could run to the habitual or occasional cab. Neither was used exclusively for the journey to work, but this was the role in which they were most susceptible to competition from the horse bus and the tram. These were cheaper, they were increasingly efficient, and by the late nineteenth century they were in competition with the private owner for horses, fodder and labour. The private carriage, as Thompson has pointed out, had become a financial burden of some weight by the last decades of the century. The hansom cab suffered like the messenger from the advent of telegraphy and the telephone. Early in the century river steamers, and to a lesser extent canal fly-boats, enjoyed some short-lived success with commuters as well as long-distance passengers, but the real alternatives to walking to work were the bus, the tram, the railway. On the whole the railways sought out this traffic reluctantly, even those eventually involved on a large scale such as the Great Eastern. Their fares were high, their stations generally on the periphery of the city centre, necessitating a walk, a cab, or a bus, and large numbers of stopping trains on lines used by more and more expresses raised considerable operating problems. The underground 'cut and cover' lines built in London from the 1850s proved over-capitalised and unremunerative (save to landowners and experts among promoters) like many main lines and were not initially oriented towards suburban traffic but to a role within the city. Here they competed, with no great success, with bus and tram; the great days of the commuter railway came with extensive electrification in the twentieth century.

The omnibus and the tram ruled supreme in the nineteenth century and proved extremely profitable. 'Not the form but the use of the vehicle . . . [was] revolutionary'[13] and even here it has its antecedents in the carrier's cart and short stage journeys in the first decades of the century; by the 1830s the horse bus was established, in the form which was to persist, providing a cheap, convenient, flexible, and profitable service over a radius of about five or six miles. On this basis the London General Omnibus Company often paid a 12½% dividend in the 1880s although by then the tram (horse, electric, or steam) had appeared as a rival. (In London however trams did not serve the central areas.) Between them in London in 1896 horse buses and trams carried almost half as many passengers again as the railways. They were particularly favoured in the last quarter of the century by falling cereal prices, their fuel costs and a large part of their current outlay. On the other hand the horse bus was unwieldy, space consuming (on the road and off it), slow, and created a noise and dirt problem (plates 22 and 23) - no Victorian novel is complete without a crossing sweeper and straw laid in the streets outside an invalid's window.

The limits of the city and its suburbs throughout the nineteenth century were very largely fixed by the horse and the pedestrian; the upper middle class might commute by rail from Brighton, the middle middle class by bus, the lower middle class by tram, the working man on foot! Some suburbs, Edmonton for example, owed almost everything to the railway, but its 'contribution to (urban) growth was shared with other more modest forms of transport to an extent often overlooked'.[14]

It was for long-distance travel, inter-city or from province to metropolis, that the railway met with most success, captured the public imagination, and made its most conspicuous impact on the landscape. Before 1850, when the railways linked almost all major towns and cities and the Railway Clearing House had ironed out practical problems resulting from a multiplicity of companies, it was quite possible to travel long distances by canal or in some cases by sea. But even at the peak of their efficiency around 1830 coaches were slow, costly, and uncomfortable; the prodigious itineraries of Dickens the journalist or Macready the actor were achieved by extreme — perhaps excessive and damaging — effort, no longer needed when the railways were operating. For members of such occupations, for businessmen and bookmakers for example, the express train was a boon; the working man neither needed it nor could afford it. If the excursion return from Leeds to the Great Exhibition was, at 5s (25p), within his means, the normal single fare of 35s

(£1.75) was not; only such special circumstances as the admittedly increasingly common move of job by the skilled man to a fairly distant city were exceptions. Nor did the railways encourage working men to take long journeys any more than to commute; even 'parliamentary' trains[15] were relatively expensive, often inconveniently timed, and sometimes the only daily third class train. Sabbatarians managed to restrict Sunday services and thus the occasional recreational journey. It is scarcely surprising that nineteenth-century expresses were small trains, four or five little coaches full of commercial travellers and boarding school pupils — two activities transformed by the railway — of maiden aunts and governesses.

At a more local level the impact of the railway was less complete. The coach and carrier's cart continued to serve country towns, some cross-country routes poorly served by the railways, and pre-eminently the railway station itself, often a new focus of growth for urban expansion. The coach proper proved very persistent; there was a London-Wendover coach as late as 1892. Likewise the carrier who sometimes turned himself into a bus and lorry owner — as did blacksmith into garage proprietor — early this century. Until the end of the century no aspect of the railway business could be carried on without horses, whether owned by the railway or meeting its needs at another's behest.

It was, as has already been noted, for recreation, for an annual or Sunday excursion, that most people were likely first to use the railway; as leisure, and the money to enjoy it, increased, so did travel. The early steamers were soon in this kind of business, on the Thames and Clyde for example — Margate received 17,000 passengers a year in 1812-13, 105,000 in 1855-6 — where they have retained this role. For the railways, and despite sabbatarian pressures, Sunday was often the busiest day for passengers — the city dweller, the Londoner especially, loved a day in the country and now he could afford and enjoy it. For a smaller section of the population the railway made possible the annual holiday, by the sea for the most part, and was thus the creator or at least the animator of many resorts. But again recreation had a pedestrian aspect; early in the nineteenth century Manchester cotton workers commonly walked to Blackpool — over 40 miles — a traffic which, formalised into 'wakes week', passed to the railways. The countryman as usual walked everywhere, and some recreations were almost universally pedestrian — courting for example. For rural recreation the safety bicycle, ousting and much improving upon the 'ordinary' (penny farthing) in the 1880s was a breakthrough towards mobility and freedom.

It is scarcely surprising that the railway established its public image and reputation in terms of the express rather than the suburban train, of the great rural engineering triumphs — Saltash Bridge, Shap summit — rather than intricate and often inconspicuous urban routes. In these former it had no rivals. Its success with holidays and excursions, its very creations, is more remarkable but it was never quite the sole agency involved. The journey to work, where its part is now taken for granted, was an area of more limited activity, the sphere primarily of pedestrian, horse, and eventually bicycle. These, and their institutional framework, set relatively restricted limits to nineteenth-century urban expansion at the same time as the railways were breaking down at least technical constraints on long-distance movement.

INFORMATION

The movement of information and ideas is less often looked at by geographers than that of goods or people, but information and ideas have to be spread and disseminated through space, and the means available for this were transformed during the nineteenth century. Specialised new technologies played their part — telegraphy, better printing presses — and so did means of distribution — the railway, and the steamer. Their effectiveness depended largely on educational advance, in particular on the elimination of illiteracy. An illiterate society is a society of individuals and groups isolated from one another except when they can meet in person or, uncertainly, through a third party: 'An illiterate maidservant living ten miles from home was cut off from her parents and her brothers and sisters far more effectively than a factory worker in Coventry is separated today from his mother and sister in Glasgow'.[16] In 1800 probably one-third of all males in England and Wales were illiterate, and an even higher proportion of females — by contrast literacy was almost the norm in Scotland. Since there were areas of relatively high literacy in England and Wales, London and the rural north for example, there were also areas of majority illiteracy, much of the rural lowland zone for example, persisting into mid-century. By 1870, the year of Forster's Education Act, four adults in five were literate and by 1900 near universal literacy had been attained, the prerequisite for communicating news, information and ideas by means of the printed word.

The conquest of illiteracy was accompanied by many other favourable circumstances like a shorter working week, higher wages and cheaper travel. Two particular aspects deserve consideration, newspapers and the Post Office, which were ranked by as shrewd a contemporary commentator as Disraeli[17] alongside the more conspicuous railway as key instruments of social change. The expansion of the newspaper industry in the second half of the century owed something to the final abolition of duties and taxes on the Press in 1855, more to the development of a largely literate public. At the same time the telegraph enabled newspapers to become more attractively up to the minute, first with home, later with foreign news. There were nine London dailies in 1830, 22 in 1865; 200 provincial dailies and weeklies in 1846 had passed 750 by 1865, an even faster rate of increase which owed something to the fact that breakfast table delivery of London dailies throughout the country became possible only at the end of the century. The coffee shop gave early nineteenth-century newspapers a wider influence than their small circulation might suggest and contemporary governments might have wished; as they attained mass circulation they turned away from their old role of political ideology and debate towards the supply of more news — local and international — and advertisement, both in bulk. Indeed it might well be argued that from being a menace to the nation's stability they turned to being a menace to its health.[18] Advertisements were not universally pernicious: they played a useful role in putting the reader in touch with the market place, in many cases much more important to him, as well as the metropolis. Nor was the specialist neglected — to cite but two examples, *The Lancet* first appeared in 1823, *The Mining Journal* in 1835.

The expansion and cheapening of postal services broadly parallels that of the Press and slightly precedes the educational revolution. The post Office quickly took to the railway and the steamer, but the creation of the Penny Post in 1840 (plate 24) followed some years of agitation and discussion. It was a dramatic abolition of bureaucracy, taxation, and geography, but as Cobden pointed out in 1841 'all . . . over-rated the immediate advantage of the change to the working class. They are too often unable to write'.[19] Nevertheless where 82 million letters were handled in 1839 there were 2,300 million by 1900. Between 1850 and 1864 delivery services were reorganised so that by the latter date 94 per cent of all letters were delivered, and delivery became a right in 1897.[20] The telegraph service was taken over by the Post Office in 1870, 25 years after it had begun and four years after it crossed the Atlantic; within two years 5,000 post offices were also telegraph offices. Telephone services were acquired more gradually – and not quite completely – between 1892 and 1911. Parcel post, for reasons already discussed, was the area of slowest development, delayed with the exception of some much abused special services, such as book and sample post, until 1883. A regional example serves to summarise progress. Thus in Rutland:

1848–13 post offices (of which 2 money order) i.e. one office to about 1,600 people.

1900–33 post offices (of which 12 money order and telegraph, only 13 purely postal) i.e. one to about 600 people.

The letter had ceased to be an event and had become a commonplace.

MONEY

'The renovation of the economy of Britain during the nineteenth century may be regarded, in one sense, as an act of continuous mobilisation of capital',[21] a movement however of which geographers have taken little notice. This mobilisation was primarily the concern of the banks, but other agencies were involved – insurance companies, even the Post Office. The Post Office Savings Bank (1861) was not only a public service but a source of government borrowing in a formerly almost untapped area.

In early nineteenth century England and Wales there was on the one hand the Bank of England, on the other numerous private banks. The law limited the number of partners in a bank to six so they were essentially local affairs, the Bank of England excepted, operating in no more than a few towns or part of a county; as yet they were by no means always detached from their mercantile or industrial origins. Banking was a growth industry, the 230 banks of 1797 had become 721 by 1810, but not a reliable one — 240 banks failed in the crisis of 1814-16. Well into the century a 'novelist could always give the story a fresh turn by bringing the local bank crashing down';[22] the City of Glasgow Bank which failed in 1878 (with unlimited liability[23]) was in fact at least a regional concern. Failure often resulted from misfortune and geographical isolation rather than mismanagement or national economic trends, so much so that a commentator in 1822 noted that 'no person in the more northern counties will take a Bank of England note if he can help it',[24] an indication of preference for the known and local over the unknown and distant. Law, local pride and practical managerial considerations all favoured local banks in the first decades of the nineteenth century. As late as 1847 difficulty of communication was the reason why the Doncaster branch of a Wakefield bank was taken over by a Doncaster firm and only exceptional concerns took the plunge into geographical extension as soon as changes in the law (1826-33) allowed banks to become joint stock companies.[25] The National Provincial, as its name implies, was among these.

Country banks were small local businesses but they needed a London bank as their agent to do their City and Bank of England business. The agent's role might be spectacular, to provide gold to a partner who had ridden or coached through the night in order that a run on the bank might be met. More important and persistent was the steady accumulation in the hands of these London banks of the funds of country banks in rural southern and eastern England, where investment opportunities were few, and their use to discount bills for banks[26] in the industrial Midlands and North where local funds fell short of local demands (figure 31). The banks were the mechanism of transfer of capital from the old rural to the new urban and industrial society, an instrument of geographical change. This capital was short-term, used to finance stocks of raw materials and finished goods in transit rather than manufacturing industry in general. Save in a few special cases, canals and railways for

Figure 31. The geographical distribution of note-issuing licences, 1822. Note the concentration in Yorkshire and the agricultural south and west. (Source: Pressnel, L.S., *Country Banking in the Industrial Revolution*, Oxford, 1956, table IX.)

example, where country banks were very active, this latter need had to be met elsewhere until late in the century. Other funds were channelled into foreign investment, creating the City's international role and Britain's continuing, albeit diminished, invisible income. Financial mechanisms and institutions changed during the century; the inter-regional flow of capital described above was crucial to economic growth early in the century but became less important as private banks gave way to joint stock and as industrial areas came to comprise the bulk of the nation's wealth. New financial agencies also possessed a regional element; the investment trusts of 1868 onwards, a means of organising British overseas investment (in North America in particular), were and are largely Scottish and particularly associated with Dundee.

The increasing importance of joint stock banks, London and provincial, and the decline in private country banking followed legislative changes in 1826-33, 1844 and 1862.[27] However these did not always favour the kinds of changes the bankers sought — fusions of country and metropolitan banks between 1844 and 1861 for example. The changed situation arose from the inadequacy of local banks in a context of rapidly expanding economic activity, and from better communications. As late as 1914 a private country banker hastened to London by train to collect gold during a crisis, but generally the railway and the telegraph made such drama unnecessary, facilitating consultation, forestalling crisis. Nevertheless banks remained relatively localised until late in the century, and inter-bank competition outside the larger towns was restrained and muted. In 1870 the average number of branches per joint stock bank was only nine, and even in 1918 the amalgamation which produced Lloyds Bank was virtually unrepresented in the north outside Tyneside.

Some comparison with the railways may be appropriate at this point. Each was a medium of communication made up of localised parts — much more so in the case of the banks — subject to some government control but not so much so as to prevent frequent calamity, the bank failure, the projected and funded but never executed railway, or even collision. Localised units gave way to regional units earlier in the railway than the banking world. Certain centralised institutions appear in mid-century — the Railway Clearing House, the Country Bankers Clearing House (1858: London banks had long possessed a clearing house) — but amalgamation into 'big four' and 'big five'[28] awaited the twentieth century and was more strongly regional in the case of the railways. The analogy is not exact but the parallels suggest that the great importance attached by geographers to the railways against the apparent insignificance of the banks, is at worst a travesty and at best an imbalance in the geography of nineteenth-century Britain.

Scottish banks were precocious by English standards. By 1800 there were already some banks with nationwide branches like the Royal Bank, the British Linen Bank (indicating its mercantile origins), as well as numerous local banks. Scottish law facilitated branch banking and favoured stability, although limited liability was adopted by banks not chartered in this form only after the 1878 catastrophe. In 1864 the largest Scottish bank with branches had no fewer than 103, the smallest nine — as many as the English average in 1870. A distinctive geography reflected a distinctive legality and an agreement on both sides not to compete across the border.

The Post Office acted as a means of financial communication (as opposed to capital mobilisation already discussed) by providing alternatives to the risky business of sending coin or notes by post. The first such, the money order, begun as a private venture by Post Office staff in 1792, was taken over in 1838 and the poundage reduced in 1840. As a result sales increased threefold. Postal Orders were created in 1883 as a cheap and simple means of transferring small sums which could be purchased (but not paid) at almost any office. How far they were used is uncertain — how, how often, how much (if at all), did rural migrants send money home?[29] — but at least a simple and nationwide service had been set up.

MARKETS AND SHOPS

The distributive apparatus of nineteenth-century Britain served a society where for the most part the seller and his wares were more mobile than the buyer, and where low wages limited the latter to a narrow range of goods and services. The itinerant pedlar or chapman, the weekly or more frequent market for perishables, the annual or occasional fair for durables met the needs of most people to a greater degree than did shops in a central place in the early nineteenth century: perhaps the manufacturer's 'tommy shop' can be considered to belong to the same class, taking goods to people on the canals and in the isolated coal and iron communities, as well as in their more usual and unfavourable light. General and specialised shops served villages and towns, but a wide range of the latter existed only in the towns and to meet middle and upper class needs. These groups had the time to go shopping, the money to pay the price of assembling and preparing a variety of products from a diversity of sources, then the essence of the grocer's trade. A number of shopkeepers such as bakers, tailers and cobblers were still producers (plate 36).

The itinerant salesman and the fair, but not the market, were beginning to lose their hold during the first half of the century. Better roads and faster coaches favoured shopkeepers and particularly the commercial traveller selling by sample. These were numerous by the 1820s and the railways, the telegraph and the penny post greatly facilitated their task and enabled them to offer better service to retailers. The market retained its role however, not only as a matter of custom and convenience, but as the best way of selling perishables. Railways and later refrigerators revolutionised some perishable trades, the supply of fresh milk for example, and enhanced the size and status of some wholesale markets,[30] but popular prejudice against chilled or frozen meat gave way but slowly and the suburban market gardener with his pony and trap enjoyed some indestructible advantages over his competitors. Markets moreover produced a municipal revenue and were popular with purchasers if not shopkeepers — further reasons for their persistence. The producer-retailer or processor-retailer was strongly entrenched in these trades and as late as 1900 the butcher was usually concerned with buying, finishing, slaughtering, and cutting — and thus with the movement of large numbers of animals into the towns — as well as with selling meat.[31]

Despite this persistence of (and some preference for) old methods there was a conspicuous retailing revolution. From 1844 in Rochdale the cooperatives provided comprehensive shops to meet working class needs. They operated in Scotland and the north in particular, and in the process also discovered the advantages of branch operation and of backward integration into production. Each was made possible by better communications and allowed better and cheaper service. Other shops soon took to the branch system, first the specialist newsagents, then — and most famously — the grocery and footwear trades, and by the 1890s the tailors. They too integrated backwards and overseas, for example Lipton's tea estates, or in some instances were a manufacturer's forward integration, as in the case of Freeman Hardy and Willis in footwear. In the process the shop became nothing more than a point of sale, dependent on railway and Post Office to link it to the factory or warehouse. On such a basis Liptons grew from one shop in 1872 to 245 in 1898, a total of 978 multiple store outlets in 1878 to 11,645 in 1900. The cooperatives alone numbered 1,400 societies and 1.7 million members (perhaps 7 million consumers) by 1900. The old-fashioned retailer was threatened, although he is not yet extinct, not only by multiples and cooperatives, which created a market as much as they competed for it, since the city centre department store (and its branches) grew rapidly, usually originating in the drapery trade, from about 1860. As their architecture so often shows their golden age came between 1880 and 1914 and depended on the creation of a substantial urban middle class market — to make their high-turnover, low-mark-up policy practicable — and on means of transport to convey purchaser and purchase — the horse bus, tram and suburban railway. In turn their specialist adaptation to mundane needs and mass markets, the 'penny bazaar', Woolworths, Marks and Spencer, had appeared by the end of the century.

By 1900 mobility had substantially passed from seller to buyer, from part-processed goods or raw materials to finished and marketable products advertised on a national basis. Railways, steamers, the parcel post, higher wages, a shorter working day and week, had enabled shop and store to triumph over pedlar and fair. The market kept much, the producer-retailer some, importance; only the supermarket remained for the twentieth century to make.

MOVEMENT AND ENVIRONMENT

The direct visual and environmental impact of the steamers, railways and canals, of a whole nineteenth-century revolution in movement and mobility, is too easily and too often exaggerated. The railways and steamers provided one base for the huge expansion of the coal and iron trades; the railways in particular captured the public imagination because of their novelty, and the conspicuously monumental character of one part of their capital investment. An ephemeral, and often flamboyantly alien labour force built embankments and excavated tunnels and cuttings on a hitherto unknown scale, dramatised by artists such as Bourne, writers such as Dickens. But even more remarkable is the speed with which abhorrence gave way to approval, and with which the railway, like the canal, merged into the rural landscape, much more so than twentieth-century motorways.

Only in the towns might the railway long remain conspicuously obtrusive (plate 7), in the cases where it had to be elevated, because it required large — and often ostentatious — terminal facilities, and because a high density of traffic made the dirt and noise problem only too evident to too many people. In any event the nineteenth-century city was both dirty and noisy, thanks to horsedrawn traffic on cobbled streets, inadequate drainage and sewerage, the factory whistle as well as its chimney, the hawker. These were not new in the nineteenth century but their scale was greatly increased. Ships and harbours had of course a localised impact, and the roads had always been there; improved surfaces were evident only at close quarters and completely new roads were few, the urban areas excepted. Telegraph, penny post, bank and multiple store had the minimal impact of the occasional new, albeit often assertive, building; only the concentrations of department stores in the West End for example late in the century represent an exception. Outside the towns then new means of movement were soon a no more than modestly obvious addition to the landscape, at most a massive bridge to rival the splendour of a medieval castle;[32] in the towns and cities of the 1870s a perceptive time traveller of the 1770s would probably not lose his way — as he so often would today — but he would certainly marvel at railways and comment on canals, shops, and the ubiquitous and variously employed horse; he would perhaps go on to put these in a wider context of growth and change.

The striking change was not the new media and their appearance but their ready acceptance as an instrument of economic and social change. Their impact had some unlikely components — the popularity of Landseer owes something to the new accessibility of the wilder and savager parts of Britain, Scotland in particular. The Queen could set up a summer residence, the middle class family take a holiday there in the railway age. The impact of a new mobility is not however restricted to exotica. An export economy assumed and depended upon means of assembling and financing imported and local raw materials and shipping manufactures; the conurbation presupposed other means of travelling to work than on foot — the bicycle, the bus, the tram, the train — and a reliable supply of cheap food (perishables included) drawn from a wide area. The repeal of the Corn Laws in 1846 and the decision to allow British farming to decay during the last quarter of the century reflected not only the existence of supplies elsewhere but of means to move them and money to pay for them. On the whole the later Victorians took all this for granted even while searching for better solutions. The social and economic inconvenience of many functionally and financially acceptable means of transport certainly led to a quest for alternatives, such as the railways themselves early in the century, later a steam engine which condensed, electric road traction and the horseless carriage (quiet and pollution free as it then appeared!) but only in a narrow sense, railway rates for example, was the adequacy of existing media challenged when economic and social problems were discussed. After all they did represent a great advance. It seems strange in the 1970s that the horseless carriage (quiet and pollution free as it then appeared!). But only given up save in a few special cases, and even more remarkable that the telephone spread so slowly. What the Victorians posessed seemed adequate to them in terms of comparison with the. past, of cost (at least in direct terms), of the needs of the times and of its ability to cope with rapid economic growth. Pressures and possibilities of radical change awaited a new century.

NOTES

1　Perkin, H., *The Age of the Railway*, Newton Abbot, 1971.
2　In a delightful inaugural lecture, *Victorian England: The Horsedrawn Society* , London, 1970.
3　First mooted in 1812: short pilot tunnels were drilled in 1881.
4　Presumably in the hope that they might contribute to profits through their consumption of food and drink?
5　Officially, if not in practice, the Channel Island packets running from Weymouth between 1794 and 1845 were simply a mail service, with passengers no more than a sideline and thus a secondary consideration.
6　Thornton, R.H., *British Shipping*, Cambridge (2nd edition), 1959, p. 64.
7　The *Oxford English Dictionary* states that the word was in colloquial use by *c.* 1880, but gives its first literary

reference as 1886.

8 There was also a phase of incomplete railway growth when some Anglo-Scottish traffic, more particularly passengers, went part way by rail and the rest by sea, e.g. London to Glasgow via Fleetwood and Ardrossan in the early 1840s.

9 Perkin, H., op.cit., p. 112.

10 ibid., p. 103.

11 The phrase was coined by Lord Bowen, a High Court judge. The date is uncertain, the judgement in which it appears being unreported, but must be between 1879 and 1894. I would like to thank Professor R.M. Caldwell for helping me to date this expression.

12 One unfortunate consequence of the existence of 'open' and 'close' villages.

13 Hibbs, J., *History of British Bus Services*, Newton Abbot, 1968, p. 29, quoting C.E. Lee.

14 Kellett, J., *The Impact of Railways on Victorian Cities*, London, 1969, p. 419.

15 In 1844 Parliament required each railway company to operate on each working day a train stopping at all stations, maintaining an average speed of not less than twelve miles per hour, composed of carriages with seats protected from the weather, and at a maximum charge of one penny per mile — the 'parliamentary' train.

16 Laslett, P., *The World we have lost*, London, 1971, pp. 205-6.

17 *Endymion*, ch. 12. The immediate context is rural Berkshire.

18 Advertisements for patent medicines — and quacks — abound, and many are so designed (and placed) in the news columns as to be a considerable nuisance to the present-day researcher. Nationwide promotion and availability of such medicines is of course another facet of the communications revolution.

19 Having given evidence before the Select Committee of 1837-8 which recommended the penny post, his subsequent comment was invited.

20 The Post Office work with which Anthony Trollope the novelist was particularly associated in his professional capacity.

21 Checkland, S.G., *The Rise of Industrial Society in England*

1815-1855 , London, 1964, p. 189.
22 Sayers, R.S., *Lloyd's Bank in the History of English Banking*, Oxford, 1957, p. 204.
23 The shareholders were liable for the bank's deficiency not merely to the extent of their own investment in its capital (limited liability, granted to banks in general − their note issue excepted − in 1862 but not commonly acted upon) but to their last penny, the reality of the case for many unfortunate shareholders in this instance.
24 Joplin, T., *On the General Principles and Present Practice of Banking in England and Scotland*, Newcastle upon Tyne, 1822, p. 545.
25 In 1826 outside a radius of 65 miles from London, in 1833 in London provided they did not issue notes.
26 The operation is explained in Sayers, R.S., *Modern Banking*, Oxford (7th edition), 1967, pp. 46-8.
27 See note 25. In 1844 note issue other than by the Bank of England (and in Scotland) was restricted (ceasing only in 1921); the 1862 legislation allowed ten partners but was otherwise restrictive.
28 Southern, Great Western, London and North-Eastern, London Midland and Scottish Railways; Barclay's, Lloyd's, Midland, Westminster, and National Provincial Banks (these last two now amalgamated, of course). There were several other quite large banks, few other railways.
29 In *Lark Rise to Candleford*, Book 3, Flora Thompson gives a classic account of a country post office in the last years of the nineteenth century. In ch. 35 there is mention of (unofficial) extension of opening hours to enable itinerant Irish labourers to purchase postal orders to send home.
30 Stratford Market in east London for example was very much the creation of the Great Eastern Railway.
31 This is still not uncommon in country towns and villages.
32 Surprisingly often in close proximity, at Newcastle upon Tyne and Conway for example.

FURTHER READING

1 OVERSEAS

Fayle, C.E., *A Short History of the World's Shipping Industry*, London, 1933.

Kirkaldy, A.W., *British Shipping*, Newton Abbot (2nd edition), 1970.

Rowland, K.T., *Steam at Sea*, Newton Abbot, 1970.

Thornton, R.H., *British Shipping*, Cambridge (2nd edition), 1959.

2 INLAND TRANSPORT

Bagwell, P.S., *The Railway Clearing House in the British Economy 1842-1922*, London, 1968.

Barker, T.C., 'Passenger transport in nineteenth century London', *Journal of Transport History*, vol. 6, 1963-4, pp. 166-74.

Barker, T.C., and Robbins, M., *A History of London Transport* (Volume 1: *The Nineteenth Century*), London, 1963.

Channon, G., 'The Aberdeenshire beef trade with London: a study in steamship and railway competition 1850-69', *Transport History*, vol. 2, 1969, pp. 1-24.

Copeland, J. *Roads and their Traffic*: 1750-1850, Newton Abbot, 1968.

Dickinson, C.G., 'Stage coach services in the West Riding of Yorkshire between 1830 and 1840', *Journal of Transport History*, vol. 4, 1959, pp. 1-11.

Dyos, H.J., and Aldcroft, D.H., *British Transport*, Leicester, 1969.

Hadfield, C.M., *British Canals*, Newton Abbot (4th ed.), 1969.

Hibbs, J., *History of British Bus Services*, Newton Abbot, 1968.

Kellett, J., *The Impact of Railways on Victorian Cities*, London, 1969.

Margetson, S.J., *Journey by Stages*, London, 1967.

Perkin, H., *The Age of the Railway*, Newton Abbot, 1971.

Perry, P.J., 'Working class isolation and mobility in rural Dorset 1837-1936: a study of marriage distances', *Institute of British Geographers: Transactions*, vol. 46, 1969, pp. 121-41.

Thompson, F.M.L., *Victorian England: The Horsedrawn Society*, London, 1970 (inaugural lecture).

Turnbull, G.L., 'The railway revolution and carrier's response:

Messrs. Pickford and Co. 1830-50', *Transport History*, vol. 2, 1969, pp. 48-71.

Williamson, G., *Wheels with Wheels*, London, 1966 (bicycles).

3   INFORMATION, MONEY AND MARKETS

Aspinall, A., 'The circulation of newspapers in the early nineteenth century', *Review of English Studies*, vol. 22, 1946, pp. 29-43.

Blackman, J., 'The development of the retail grocery trade in the nineteenth century', *Business History*, vol. 9, 1967, pp. 110-17.

Burnett, J., 'The baking industry in the nineteenth century', *Business History*, vol. 5, 1962, pp. 98-105.

Davis, D., *A History of Shopping* London, 1966.

Jefferys, J.B. *Retail Trading in Britain 1850-1950*, Cambridge, 1954.

Kellett, E.E., 'The Press', in Young, G.M., *Early Victorian England*, London, 1934, vol. 2, pp. 1-98.

Paserunadjian, H., *The Department Store*, London, 1954.

Pressnell, L.S., *Country Banking in the Industrial Revolution*, Oxford, 1956.

Robinson, H., *Britain's Post Office*, London, 1953.

Sayers, R.S., *Lloyd's Bank in the History of English Banking*, Oxford, 1957.

Stone, L., 'Literacy and education in England 1640-1900', *Past and Present*, vol. 42, 1969, pp. 69-139.

Sutton, G.B., 'The marketing of ready made footwear in the nineteenth century', *Business History*, vol. 6, 1964, pp. 93-112.

Sykes, J., *The Amalgamation Movement in English Banking 1825-1924*, London, 1926.

Taylor, A.M., *Gillet's: Bankers at Banbury and Oxford*, Oxford, 1964.

Wadsworth, A.P., 'Newspaper circulation 1800-1954', *Transactions of the Manchester Statistical Society*, 1955, pp. 1-40.

7 The Agricultural Interest: Change and Decay

The landowner, the farmer and the labourer usually make their appearance in one of the earlier chapters of any book dealing with past economies and societies. For much of the past such priority is defensible, serving to emphasise the key role of the land in pre-industrial society, but for the nineteenth century, when the pre-eminence of agriculture is markedly on the wane, this priority is less desirable, for however well qualified, it serves to give the reader an exaggerated sense of the importance of farming. Agriculture was pre-eminent in 1800; landowners dominated parliament, farmers the countryside. Over 2,000,000 farmers and farm labourers were the largest occupational group. Only in mid-century did the greater part of Britain's population cease to live in the countryside, and by 1900 agriculture was small beer by comparison with cotton or coal. The contrast lay not so much in terms of occupied space – 85 per cent of the land was still farmed or grazed, albeit often very badly – or even employment, but in terms of contribution to the economy, and above all to exports, to prosperity, and in public esteem. In a society built upon booming export industries agriculture eventually and inevitably became an industry depressed by competitive imports. There were times when agriculture occupied the centre of the stage – the years culminating in Corn Law repeal in 1846 for example – or enjoyed great prosperity as in the 1850s and 1860s, but for the most part the century witnessed the removal of agriculture from a dominant to a subsidiary socio-economic position, from simple and assured prosperity to a state of adversity which could be countered only by enterprise and ingenuity. In general the agricultural interest retired in good order and periods of rout never lasted more than two or three

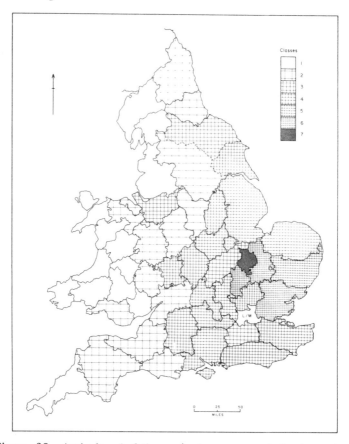

Figure 32. Agricultural failures (assignments and bankruptcies, annual average by counties) 1881-83 as a percentage of the farming population in 1881: 1, less than 0.1%; 2, 0.1% to 0.2%; 3, 0.2% to 0.3%; 4, 0.3% to 0.4%; 5, 0.4% to 0.5%; 6, 0.5% to 0.6%; 7, more than 0.6%; L/M, London and Middlesex. (Source: Perry, P.J., *British Farming in the Great Depression 1870-1914*, Newton Abbot, fig. 1.)

years even in the severe depression of the last quarter of the century (figures 32 and 33). Only in a very few years did agriculture's contribution to the national income diminish. But it was a withdrawal, relative rather than absolute, from prosperity to penury, from prestige to powerlessness.

A sequential typology – Napoleonic prosperity, postwar depression, the splendours of mid-century 'high farming' and the 'great depression' – is commonly used when British farming

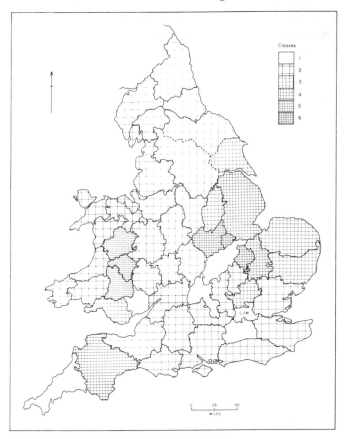

Figure 33. Agricultural failures 1881-83 (a) in relation to agricultural failures 1871-73 (b), (a/b): 1, less than 1.5; 2, 1.5 to 3.0; 3, 3.0 to 4.5; 4, 4.5 to 6.0; 5, 6.0 to 7.5; 6, more than 7.5; L/M, London and Middlesex). Note the general evenness of the incidence of failure compared to figure 32; the high values in some western counties relating to epidemics. (Source: as figure 32, figure 4).

in the nineteenth century is being considered, sometimes with the addition of a third short but severe depression following on Corn Law repeal. The general validity of such an approach can scarcely be questioned, but it requires qualification at almost all points. The prosperity of mid-century for example conceals problems which engendered a shift towards pastoral farming and thus anticipated the depression. A regional approach affords no better solution to these problems, important though regional differences were and local studies are. It is more appropriate to consider firstly the context of change, the forces which were at work and the circumstances in which they acted, and then to examine the changes themselves.

THE CONTEXT OF CHANGE

A rapidly increasing and, for much of the century, increasingly wealthy population provided the most favourable feature of the environment in which the agricultural interest worked. More people had to be fed, and while debate continues as to their standard of living in the first half of the century[1] and certainly while the consumer of 1900 was not the consumer of the 1970s, there is no doubt that the British were much better fed in 1900 than in 1800. Farmers whose products either entered the average man's diet during the century or were transformed from occasional luxuries to everyday necessities were particularly favoured. Thus the dairy farmer, the horticulturalist, even the grazier, prospered more than the traditional arable farmer. Ironically the farmer's preference for engagement in cereal cropping remained very strong, a preference based on habit and social esteem rather than economic returns, a persistent and widespread belief that to be a farmer was to grow corn.[2] By comparison the traditional view, particularly strongly entrenched in wartime conditions early in the century, that Britain must try to feed itself gave way almost imperceptibly to an assumption that a much more populous Britain could and would be fed by the world at large; fears of Napoleonic power gave way to fulmination against high prices, and these to faith in the Pax Brittanica. A larger and richer populace not only ate more food, it occupied more land. By comparison with the present-day situation this competition for space was modest and uncontrolled; but London did spread over the market gardens of Putney and Fulham, Leblanc alkali works devasted Cheshire farms, the new laird's fashionable recreation replaced sheep with grouse or deer. On the whole, population increase favoured the farmer, but not necessarily the British farmer since it took a form which divorced an increasingly large proportion of the population from contact with or understanding of the farming interest and the countryside and its problems. Rural Britain became not the nation's larder but its leisure; the countryman of whatever class was no longer the supplier of essential goods but an anachronism or an irrelevance, be he a reputedly powerful — even wicked — vested interest, an earl or a mere esquire, or a popular subject of derision — toothless and unlettered Hodge.[3]

Nineteenth-century agriculture operated in a legal as well as a demographic framework. Every section of the rural community was subject to legal constraints (and incentives) and to legal intervention; in the century of *laissez faire* these remained somewhat biased in favour of property, maintaining the landlord in a stronger position than his tenant, the farmer than his labourer. This bias was however to be largely broken down if not wholly destroyed by means of agricultural legislation. Some of these laws represented the continuance of an existing situation. In 1800 enclosure by Act of Parliament had been the norm for a century, albeit constantly undergoing modification, and machinery allowing for enclosure without each scheme coming before the legislature was devised only when the process was almost complete.[4] The Napoleonic War witnessed one of the high-water marks of enclosure, both of open fields, in the Midlands in particular, and of wastes and moors, a consequence of high prices and fears for the nation's food supply. Thereafter the nearly but never quite completed operation quickly slackened. Enclosure Acts dealt with property, the Corn Laws with prices — another area of long standing concern.[5] Their repeal marks both the triumph of free trade and the end of a tradition of economic regulation extending back to the Middle Ages. Political and technological circumstance however muted the impact of repeal for nearly 30 years.

In the middle of the century a new legislative pattern emerges, that of selective intervention which, after nearly a century of half-hearted application, transformed British farming from the 1930s. Peel's Public Money Drainage Act of 1846 and its successors encouraged and subsidised the application of a new technology, pipe drains, as well as acting as a modest sop to offended landowners and farmers. The Agricultural Holdings Acts, of 1883 in particular, ventured to control landlord and tenant relationships, to take away some traditional (landlord) property rights, in the contentious area of the tenant's right to be compensated for the improvements he had made during his tenancy on giving up a farm. The 'whisky money' of 1890,[6] produced by abortive government action in one area, ended up financing agricultural education. In short the conspicuous termination of one kind of legislative support in 1846 is followed by the modest initiation of another kind, more selective and localised, and for a century inadequately protective, but eventually a more satisfactory basis for the prosperity of British farming.

Farming exists not only under the law and to meet the consumers' needs but also in terms of the aspirations of several groups. The largest of these, the public at large, might have summed up their wishes in the phrase 'cheap food', to find them satisfied by the events of 1846 and more generally by an improved agricultural technology. The interests of farmer, landowner and labourer were, in their own view, less satisfactorily met; nor were they wholly economic and rational, each embracing a deal of custom and even ignorance. Nevertheless by 1900 a much greater part of Britain's farming was run as a business than in 1800. The railways, education — both general and technical — hard times, shows and societies, had contributed to a great commercialisation, a realisation that profitable farming now called for the matching — even the measurement — of inputs and outputs. Commercialisation was also one aspect of the rural exodus, of surplus (and often ambitious) labourers, of incompetent or unlucky farmers, of inept or spendthrift landlords. The Victorian belief in progress *per se* was undoubtedly a further element in commercialisation, but progress for progress' sake, so popular in mid-century, could run counter to profitability, a necessary if not total objective for farmer and landlord. Lavish expenditure on drainage, of heavy land in particular, was fashionable and 'progressive' in mid-century, a hallmark of 'high farming'; it often gave a meagre return on capital or none at all. New cottages (plate 26), new branch railway lines in rural areas, had more social than directly economic justification. Some rural fashions were blatantly anti-agricultural, the shooting of the hand-reared pheasant and the hardy Scottish grouse, and even, to a lesser degree, fox-hunting. This was even more the case when management passed out of the hands of resident landowners and their tenants.[7] The personnel of nineteenth-century farming is then an integral part of its context, not merely a statistical background but thousands of individuals, extraordinary or everyday in their behaviour. It is essential to ask, if not always to answer, such questions as what did they want? what could they afford? how well informed were they?

New technologies within agriculture and outside it provided the most conspicuous group of forces for change, and perhaps those most likely to be misunderstood. Not only is there the question of terminology — technology is not synonymous with mechanisation — but of scale of impact. Some of the most evident innovations were among the least important — steam-ploughing — some of the least conspicuous the most significant — ley-farming. Some can be dated with precision, at least as far as their direct impact on farming is concerned, although all have antecedents and all required time for their spatial diffusion: a machine for making cheap drainpipes (1835), the invention of basic slag (1878), the concept of the separation of the maintenance ration and the production ration of the dairy cow (1887) belong in this category.[8] Other innovations spread more slowly, the swede early in the century for example, the use of oil cake as a feed for cattle. The area of least spectacular progress was mechanisation, the substitution of power tools for hand tools in particular. The binder was commonplace by 1900, the farming journals of mid-century advertised clod crushers and chaff cutters, but cheap labour, small fields (often pronouncedly ridged) and above all the absence of a conveniently mobile source of power inhibited progress. The mechanical revolution awaited the internal combustion and diesel engines. New technology cost money, landlord's money or tenant's money, and though at times and in certain parts of the country this was abundantly — even excessively — forthcoming (in mid-century and much of East Anglia for example), elsewhere it was not, in the post Napoleonic depression, in remote Wales and southwest England where labour was abundant.

New technologies directly applicable on the farm were paralleled by developments outside farming. Railways and factory methods, albeit rudimentary, made drainpipes and superphosphate cheaply and widely available; when fat cattle and milk could be sent by train to the city the drover and often the cheesemaker were out of business. But technology had a less happy side where farming was concerned: the steamer and the railway flooded the country with cheap grain, the refrigerator was not yet a household convenience but it quickly brought an end to the protection provided by nature for the British farmer's perishable produce, meat and even milk.[9] New methods might lower prices as well as costs, increase competition as well as production. Prices and costs were what mattered most to the farmer; to the landlord they were filtered through rents and through investment and maintenance programmes, and to the labourer wages and living costs were a sphere of interaction largely beyond his control. But to the farmer, whatever his aims and aspirations, ability to maintain a differential between ever-changing costs and ever-changing returns by means of skilful application of technology was essential if he was to stay in business.

How a farmer stayed in business, and for that matter how the landlord did so and whether the labourer left the land, was a matter of individual decision, of a personal response to the multitude of circumstances outlined above. In this respect farming was very different from most other industries, and particularly from those which were developing most rapidly — coal and iron for example; all farmers, to say nothing of landowners, in all some hundreds of thousands, were policy makers and policy executants. Geography combined with personality to decide how forces for change would be applied. Some were universally applicable, so that an understanding of the separate roles of maintenance and production rations was as meaningful in Kent as in Kirkcudbright. Others were universal in theory but localised in practice — loans for land drainage were widely available but relevant only where drainage was a problem and one which appeared to be potentially soluble; enclosure was complete in many areas before 1800. The largest group of possibilities was geographically the most constrained, thus a new railway opened the urban milk market only to willing farmers within pony and trap distance of a station and the swede, although a response to the environmental shortcomings of the turnip, could not be grown everywhere; new rotations had to match soil and climate as well as costs and prices. Traditionally and actually British farming was environmentally adjusted. Farmers grew wheat, beans, fallow in rotation on the heavy undrained clays because experience showed that no other system worked. It is certainly a perceptive view of nineteenth-century developments which comments that 'the progress of farming technology reduced a farmer's dependence on environmental conditions'; to go on to relate this to 'a declining regional differentiation',[10] as Grigg does, is to venture on to less safe ground, at least outside South Lincolnshire and in the second half of the century. New methods and the circumstances in which they were applied were on the one hand matched to particular tasks or problems and on the other constantly changing; they thus combined as often to enhance as to diminish regional differences. Some periods — mid-century for example — certainly witnessed both an evening-up of standards, the worst coming closer to the best, and widespread imitation of particular techniques, such as oil cake as a cattle feed to produce manure. Other periods saw the reverse, for depression in the last quarter of the century generated both intensive horticulture and 'dog and stick' farming,[11] rendering every advantage of environment, position, and individual skill more rather than less important, thus engendering a higher degree of local and regional variation.

Lastly it is necessary to recall that there were some relatively unchanging elements in the rural scene. Some farms remained more remote than others, some presented more intractable environments, facts which could be modified but not overturned. Rural Britain remained a society and economy of landlord and tenant, the former made up of private individuals and also of corporate bodies such as Cambridge colleges and cathedral chapters. Legislation, public debate, even political agitation did little to change this situation — owner-occupiers remained a small minority. Similarly British agriculture remained an amalgam of large, medium, and small farms but with scarcely a peasant in sight — again this issue from time to time captured public interest and attention, but attempts to establish a peasantry were localised and unsuccessful.[12] The apparent scale of values within farming remained unaltered: arable farming and grazing were fit occupations for a gentleman, a status more and more aspired to by farmers — perhaps under pressure from their wives — during the century, dairying and market gardening were not.

THE CHARACTERISTICS OF CHANGE

Change is of the essence of farming. In most of the world the basis of farming is to exploit a not wholly reliable seasonal cycle as well as a more predictable physical environment both changing sharply over short distances and short periods of time in some cases. There are also frequent and often cumulative adjustments, alterations in practice based on hindsight but which masquerade as foresight; the most hidebound farmer cannot proceed on absolutely identical lines in successive years. Thirdly there are major innovations, the decision to adopt a new crop rotation, to give up pigs, to buy a new implement, merging gradually however into the second 'adjustment' category. Too often only the third of these categories above is considered by scholars, less spectacular considerations are neglected; undoubtedly the overall scale of values is correct, but not to the exclusion of seasons and minor adjustments from all consideration. Moreover the analytical framework which is now widely and aptly employed in considering the process of agricultural innovation — knowledge, decision, action, obstacles, adoption, effects — serves to perpetuate assumptions of this kind.

The farmer exploits the seasonal cycle, he also endures it, and in the nineteenth century did so without the wealth of technology now available as a counter-measure. The weather — the context of farming — was not only intractable and unpredictable but at times an agent of change. Runs of good seasons bred complacency, but more conspicuously adverse seasons, in the late 1870s for example, might both contribute to a crisis by raising costs, reducing yields or decimating sheep flocks, and at the same time serve to mask more fundamental long-term trends.[13] Moreover this particular crisis was both regionally and locally variable. The process of minor adjustment represents an alternative unspectacular process of change which may be at least as important as that of deliberate innovation; highland Britain displays not only the geometry of large-scale enclosure early in the nineteenth century but the small irregular patterns of protracted informal reclamation; the increase in the grassland acreage in late nineteenth-century Britain owed as much or more to a host of little decisions (or indecisions) — not to plough this field, to allow that rotation pasture to run on —

as to deliberate policies to move into grassland farming and lay down permanent pasture.

The most important of all the changes which took place in British agriculture during the nineteenth century had both an innovation and an adjustment component. It was the continuation of the extension of the cultivated acreage, a matter of which the legitimacy in terms of 'agricultural revolution' has been contentiously debated but of which the role in sustaining both eighteenth- and nineteenth-century population increase can scarcely be gainsaid.[14] Early in the century the Napoleonic Wars favoured enclosure of moors, wastes and open fields, and the process continued throughout the century even into the 'great depression'. The margin of cultivation ebbed and flowed but reclamation was never completely halted. In the Fens meres and wastes were drained, Whittlesey and Deeping for example, and the operation of extension merges imperceptibly into that of drainage, so characteristic of heavy land in mid-century, so vigorously debated a hundred years later.[15]

Areal extension embraced not only new land in Britain but also new land overseas, not only outputs but also inputs. Englishmen came to be fed on the wheat of the prairies, the lambs of the Canterbury Plains; the 'high farmer' needed oil cake from the Baltic, guano from Peru. This extension was dependent on discovery, and also upon technology. It contained elements beneficial to the British farmer but others which were to prove his ruin. The resources of the New World bankrupted not a few farmers and landowners (figure 34). In brief an agricultural economy operating on an insular base in 1800, aspiring to occasional export, employing a small range of imports, was in the deep end of a worldwide economy by 1900, an areal extension of greater importance than its own efforts to find more land within its own island limits.

Nineteenth-century farmers were not generally accustomed to think in terms of productivity, and yet this was an area where they were conspicuously successful. Output increased almost continuously, the nation's farmers were still providing the bulk of its food supply in 1900 while employing less labour and less capital. Productivity per unit of labour was a particularly successful area: a large part of the agricultural interest, some 700,000 men, left the land without great social distress, an adverse impact on output, or even a spectacular

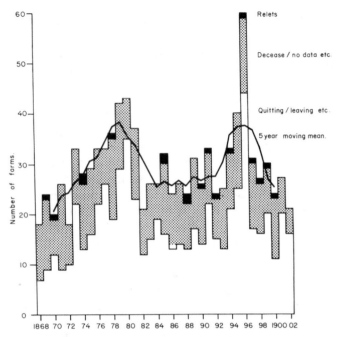

Figure 34. Character of farm sales in Huntingdonshire 1868-1902.
The two peaks in the moving mean correspond to the two periods of
acutest depression. (Source: *Peterborough Advertiser*.)

mechanisation, although the improved hand tool was undoubtedly an important factor. Farming had been grossly overmanned, its labour force had been inefficient, underpaid and underfed in southern and eastern England in particular (figure 35). From mid-century this situation, wage differentials excepted, markedly improved. Methods for improving productivity per acre or per beast developed through the century, but to a greater degree than improved labour productivity their adoption depended upon knowledge, willingness to apply them, and finance for their implementation. There were times when it paid to farm less well; the technical brilliance of mid-century high farming did not make money in the 1880s and 1890s. Some new methods however almost guaranteed a good return, such as open-field enclosure and application of basic slag to worn out pastures. Productivity per unit of capital — the farmer's return on his investment — was less assuredly on the increase during the century; it was a century of investment, of growing

(high wages)

PASTORAL

(high rent)

ARABLE

(low rent)

(low wages)

Figure 35. The basic divisions of mid-century British farming as viewed by an expert of the period, James Caird. After 35 unprosperous years the predominantly arable area is at its minimum extent. (Source: Caird, J., *English Agriculture 1850-51*, London, 1852, frontispiece.)

awareness that farming was a business of inputs and outputs, but at times, after 1815 and in the last quarter of the century in particular, a great deal of capital had to be written off. It was often the areas of highest investment — eastern England and the Midlands — which proved most vulnerable, high investment necessitating high prices. Investment tended to be only as profitable as the predictive powers of the investor were reliable. Much mid-century investment, drains and even permanent pasture, paid its way only for a few years, likewise much upland enclosure early in the century, but vegetables, fruit trees and heated glass-houses late in the century paid handsomely. So much depended on management and on timing, and thus on the individual. What were his possible choices?

The landowner was concerned on the one hand with rents and on the other with long-term investment. In each area he was constrained; social considerations[16] made it much easier to lower rents quickly in a crisis than to raise them in a boom, except in parts of the highland zone, and the strict family settlement[17] sometimes inhibited development. Investment was also related to the level of rents, other sources of income and, not least, the personal interest and inclination of the landowner. Enclosure and buildings (plate 27) were traditionally the most important areas of landlord activity, matched by his less tangible and financial exemplary and educative role. By mid-century draining had largely replaced enclosure; late in the century investment was generally but by no means invariably cut back, so too was maintenance, another and often neglected aspect of the landlord's role. The countryside became dilapidated and a few landlords took the ultimate step of selling their estates.

The tenant farmer had a great deal more room for manoeuvre than his landlord, and for that matter the owner-occupier. He was much less in the public eye and could harry and pester his landlord in a way which was unthinkable in the reverse direction. He could move in and out of business, if not easily at least with some flexibility. What was hardest for him was to change everyday practice; attention is rightly and necessarily focused on innovators but they were always a minority, their reluctant and tardy imitators the silent majority. Innate conservatism, limited education, finance and everyday routine inhibited change. So too did geographical considerations; there were always more options open, in good times and bad, to the farmer on a light loam near a big city than to the unfortunate tenant of a heavy clay farm seven miles from the railway. In fact the farmer's most basic decision − corn or horn? − was to some degree made for him by his location. There were few alternatives to pastoral farming in the highland zone although the railways expanded the range of possibilities from stores to fat beasts and dairying, and also made for cheaper fertiliser and easier migration. On the whole farmers in these areas were at the mercy not only of a tough environment but of limited outlets −

the purchasers of store sheep and cattle in English markets, dairy companies, and butchers — although in a few favoured localities, Lancashire and South Wales for example, industrialisation provided booming local markets. In hard times however there was often no alternative to tighter belt and shorter purse other than to give up,[18] perhaps to emigrate.

It was in Midland England and lowland eastern Scotland that horn and corn were most meaningful alternatives. Within the framework of high farming, intensive and integrated arable and livestock husbandry, and underpinned by improvements in drainage — the removal of a major environmental constraint — these two regions oscillated between emphasis upon livestock and grain. If popular preference was for the latter, less demanding of capital and everyday attention, and which long continued to be thought of as the paying side of the business when manifestly it had ceased to be so, price movements in the long run favoured the livestock side. As beef and mutton paid better than wheat and barley, farmers reluctantly kept more stock — a costly investment — fed off more of their corn, and put more land to permanent pasture or feed crops. Primarily arable high farming retreated eastwards. Parts of the Midlands had a long-standing pastoral reputation, Leicestershire for example, but such pastures were not easily made; much of what went under the name in the last quarter of the century was more weed than seed. Temporary grass had a long history — it is no more than another name for the convertible husbandry of the classical agricultural revolution; the nineteenth-century contribution, particularly associated with the Scottish borders, was to devise new systems and to show how to exploit their full potential.[19] There were also opportunities for dairying, in Derbyshire and Staffordshire for example, and for market gardening, as raspberries in Lanarkshire, but the Midlands and central Scotland remained pre-eminently the domain of adjustable mixed farming.

In eastern England this system ran into problems in sustaining grass through often hot, dry summers, on light and infertile soils in particular. Temporary grass was particularly prone to fail; permanent pasture was — wrongly — thought to be impossible. The arable element predominated, the livestock were mere manure machines. It required hard times to demonstrate alternatives, such as supplying London with winter milk from cattle fed on roots in the north Essex clays. Alderman Mechi's high farming was eventually his ruin,[20] but Tiptree fruit and Wisbech strawberries proved rewarding enterprises. In East Anglia, and more widely, traditional views as to profitable farming had given way to new ideas, themselves made practicable by the railways and by rising urban incomes.

The labourer's decision was to stay or to move. Low wages, rural under-employment, poor housing and a tradition of subservience all encouraged the labourer — or more often his children — to move when opportunity presented itself. The railways, universal education and hard times for farming in the last quarter of the century facilitated mobility, even within the 'farming ladder' (plate 28). The process was not of redundancy but of non-replacement, not, with some exceptions, of a direct exodus to mills and mines but, as been noted, of a drift to larger villages and country towns, the first leg of the stepwise migration process. The girls went to domestic service, the men to the railways, the police, the armed forces, or to use rural skills as urban carters and carriers. The lower echelons of the service sector depended on a flow of recruits from the cottages as much as the upper ranks looked to the younger sons from hall and rectory.

Until about the 1860s every circumstance favoured that increasing uniformity of farming practice, at least within lowland Britain, noted by Grigg. The economic base appeared secure, mixed arable-livestock farming paid well, tools such as superphosphate and tile drains were available and could be afforded to counter environmental problems. Already a number of circumstances favouring diversity were at work in the highland zone — railways and industrialisation at the farm gate. It took the hard times which followed 1875 to bring back diversity to the lowland zone: on the one hand the means to conquer the environment could no longer be afforded, on the other difficulties were best overcome by adaptive exploitation of any environmental and locational advantage. Everywhere there were several possible solutions, although many farmers found none of them; overall the answer was a greener and better fed Britain in 1900 than in 1800, a greater diversity of farming practice but not necessarily a higher technical standard than half a century earlier.

NOTES

1 See particularly the writings of R.M. Hartwell and E.J.E. Hobsbawm.
2 See for example Street, A.G., *Farmer's Glory*, London, 1932, where the personal problems of changing from arable farming to dairying in the 1920s are well discussed.
3 The general tendency to regard all landowners as at least potentially wicked, all farm labourers as idiots, is manifest in a variety of ways in the nineteenth century. The rustic of the *Punch* cartoon is almost always a half-wit, and in W.S. Gilbert's words 'All baronets are bad' (*Ruddigore*, Act 1).
4 Notably the General Enclosure Act 1845.
5 Hence too the fact that grain prices alone appeared in the *London Gazette*.
6 So called because it was originally voted as part of a scheme for licensing reform; the scheme fell through but the compensation which was to have been paid was used for educational ends.
7 Damage to crops by game was a constant source of friction between farmers and landlords, even after the Ground Game Act of 1880 strengthened the farmer's position. The few complaints about hunting probably reflect the fact that farmers could take part in this sport whereas shooting was generally reserved for the landowner.
8 That is that the dairy cow requires a basic ration to keep alive, the supply of food over and above this level determining the flow of milk.
9 Fresh milk was occasionally imported from France late in the century. The refrigerated trade in perishable milk products, especially butter from New Zealand, was much more important.
10 Grigg, D.B., *The Agricultural Revolution in South Lincolnshire*, Cambridge, 1966, p. 186.
11 That is extensive grazing for which the only tools needed were a dog and a stick.
12 In both instances agitation was commonplace in the last two decades of the century, and commonly completely oblivious of the realities of agricultural depression.
13 In this case tending to make farmers think that their misfortunes were purely caused by exceptional seasons and

would thus right themselves.
14 See the debate between G.E. Mingay and E. Kerridge in *Agricultural History*, 1969.
15 Summarised by Whetham, E.H., 'Sectoral advance in English agriculture 1850-80: a summary', *Agricultural History Review*, vol. 16, 1968, pp. 46-8.
16 In particular the fact that most English landlords lived on their estates for at least part of the year alongside their tenants, went to church and rode to hounds with them, and commonly hoped to exert a political influence over them.
17 The system whereby to ensure that the estate was handed down more or less intact from generation to generation the owner surrendered his rights as proprietor and became tenant for life. The subject is very complex.
18 Hence the importance of migrant Scots or Welsh farmers from overcrowded districts in England at some periods. See Smith, E.L., *Go East for a Farm*, Oxford, 1932.
19 By 1907 the fourth edition of the classic of the subject, Elliot, R.H., *The Agricultural Changes required by these times*, Kelso, 1898 had been renamed *The Clifton Park System of Farming*.
20 Mechi used the fortune derived from his 'magic razor strop' to reclaim Tiptree Heath from 1841. He wrote many books on farming.

FURTHER READING

1 GENERAL AND REGIONAL

Chambers, J.D., and Mingay, G.E., *The Agricultural Revolution*, London 1966.
Fussell, G.E., *The English Dairy Farmer 1500-1900*, London, 1952.
Fussell, G.E., *The Farmer's Tools 1500-1900*, London, 1952.
Gaskell, P., *Morvern Transformed: A Highland Parish in the Nineteenth Century*, Cambridge, 1968.
Grigg, D.B., *The Agricultural Revolution in South Lincolnshire*, Cambridge, 1966.
Kerr, B., *Bound to the Soil: a social history of Dorset 1750-1918*, London, 1968.
Symon, J.A., *Scottish Farming Past and Present*, Edinburgh,

1959.

Thirsk, J., and Imray, J., *Suffolk Farming in the Nineteenth Century,* Suffolk Record Society, Ipswich, 1958.

Thompson, F.M.L., *English Landed Society in the Nineteenth Century,* London, 1963.

Trow-Smith, R., *A History of British Livestock Husbandry 1700-1900,* London, 1959.

2 EARLY NINETEENTH CENTURY

Adams, L.P., *Agricultural Depression and Farm Relief in England 1813-1852,* London, 1932.

Hunt, H.G., 'Agricultural rent in south-east England 1788-1825', *Agricultural History Review,* vol. 7, 1959, pp. 98-108.

John, A.H., 'Farming in war time 1793-1815', in Jones, E.L., and Mingay, G.E., *Land, Labour and Population in the Industrial Revolution,* London, 1967.

Martin, J.M., 'The parliamentary enclosure movement and rural society in Warwickshire', *Agricultural History Review,* vol. 15, 1967, pp. 19-39.

Tate. W.E., *The English Village Community and the Enclosure Movement,* London, 1967.

3 HIGH FARMING IN MID-CENTURY

Caird, J.B., *English Agriculture in 1850-51,* London, 1852 and subsequent reprints.

Collins, E.T.J., and Jones, E.L., 'Sectoral advance in English agriculture 1850-80', *Agricultural History Review,* vol. 15, 1967, pp. 65-81. (In reply to Sturgess, R.W., cited below).

Darby, H.C., 'The Draining of the English Clay-lands', *Geographische Zeitschrift,* vol. 52, 1964, pp. 190-201.

Hunt, E.H.; 'Labour productivity in British agriculture 1850-1914', *Economic History Review,* 2nd series, vol. 29, 1967, pp. 280-92.

Jones, E.L., 'The changing basis of English agricultural prosperity, 1853-1873', *Agricultural History Review,* vol. 10, 1962, pp. 102-19.

Phillips, A.D.M., 'Underdraining and the English claylands 1850-80: a review', *Agricultural History Review,* vol. 17, 1969, pp. 44-55.

Sturgess, R.W., 'The Agricultural Revolution on the English

Clays', *Agricultural History Review*, vol. 14, 1966, pp. 104-121. Also 'A rejoinder', *Agricultural History Review*, vol. 15, 1967, pp. 82-7 (Replying to Collins, E.J.T., and Jones, E.L.).

Whetham, E.H., 'Sectoral advance in English agriculture 1850-80: a summary', *Agricultural History Review*, vol. 16, 1968, pp. 46-8.

4 LATE NINETEENTH-CENTURY 'DEPRESSION'

Haggard, H.R., *Rural England*, London, 1906.

Hall, A.D., *A Pilgrimage of British Farming*, London, 1913.

Perry, P.J., *British Farming in the Great Depression 1875-1914*, Newton Abbot, 1974.

8 Britain in 1900:
The Limits of Prosperity

The reputation which the first decade of the twentieth century still enjoys as a golden age owes something to the subsequent holocaust, but it is also derived from a real renewal of prosperity after 20 years of intermittent depression. Times had begun to improve before 1900, itself a very good year, and between 1896 and 1913 exports doubled in value and imports increased by more than half. But perhaps rather ominously the export boom was led by the old staples, coal and steel, rather than by new lines, and it is arguable that enthusiastic overseas investment and involvement served primarily to deprive British industry of the capital and manpower it needed for modernisation. The geographer concerned with this period is then writing of a boom compounded and complicated by a subsequent tragedy. He is able however to call to his aid a mass of evidence collected and analysed by the many social investigators of a period when 'the attention of the general public has been more directed, probably, to economic and industrial problems, to varying social conditions than ever before'.[1] Evidence of a quickened interest in the state of the nation, these investigations themselves reveal an important aspect of the 'geosophy'[2] of the period, an awareness that in the richest nation and society in the world there existed great social problems of which the geographical characteristics were of basic significance, be they a slum courtyard or an impoverished village. These objective surveys are parallelled by more partisan endeavours, at worst polemic, describing the ills and evils of the nation as a political consequence and for a political purpose; the writings of Masterman and his associates are probably the most significant examples of this genre. Of equal importance but much less widely known or read is Mackinder's *Britain and the British Seas* (1902), the first and incomparably the best modern geography of Britain, an enormous intellectual advance over even the English volume of the *Géographie Universelle* of 1886,[3] and soon to be imitated and influential in a number of county geographies. Victorian self-assurance gave way during no more than a generation to Edwardian self-scrutiny, 'the uneasy feeling . . . that the nineteenth century, which has done such wonderful things, and from which things so much more wonderful were hoped, has been on the whole a failure'.[4] Such an introspective mood sets the scene and provides the framework for this concluding chapter of an historical geography which of necessity anticipates much of the geography of 1900 in its central chapters. What were the geographical problems to be faced and found in early twentieth-century Britain? What were the geographical elements in the transformation of Britain which few would deny had taken place since 1800?

By 1900 Britain was already having to adjust to a status in world affairs — a new political geography — less lofty and certainly less lonely than in mid-century. The internantional prestige and self-confidence of Britain was as yet scarcely touched, even by the misadventures of the Boer War, but economic power and authority had waned considerably, at least on a comparative scale, since the 1870s. Not only were there other producers of the wide range of goods, and at least some of the services, which Britain had supplied to much of the world during the nineteenth century, notably Germany and the U.S.A., but they were often more competitive. As has been mentioned already there is no reason to believe that Britain's mid-century worldwide commercial dominance could have persisted, but successful foreign competition served not only to demonstrate this fact but to generate both political rivalries and realignments. Foreign successes were also taken to reflect upon Britain's social structures in general, educational shortcomings in particular, and upon the experience of half a century of free trade in a world of foreign competitors, foreign tariffs, and a large empire. The geographical re-evaluation implicit in the term 'little Englander' was as yet exceptional, but commercial and political imperialism and protectionism, another new geography were commonplace. Britain's place in the geography of world trade, and thus of world power, was altogether a matter for revision by the end of the century.

Within Britain the principal focus of attention and concern was the cities. Since mid-century Britain had been more an urban than a rural society and for considerably longer had been the most urbanised nation in the world. One great nineteenth-century achievement was to house this rapidly growing urban population, but when the achievement has been admitted there remains the undoubted existence of appalling problems, rural as well as urban, in this area. They presented themselves to educated Edwardians almost as forcefully as they pressed upon their unfortunate proletarian victims. These problems 'were less those of economic depression than of a prosperity unevenly shared'.[5] Charles Booth discovered and publicised the fact that in the richest country in the world a third of the population endured chronic poverty. In 1891 three-fifths of the population of Glasgow, at the apogee of its economic power and prestige, lived in overcrowded conditions[6] and even in London, away from the Scottish tradition of tenement housing and with a less cyclical economic base, the figure was one in five. The Boer War publicised the consequences of this situation when in 1899 three recruits in every five at Manchester proved to be physically unfit even under drastically reduced wartime stand-ards'.[7]

Poverty, physique, and housing were evidently related, albeit regionally variable, problems. They do not exhaust such a list. Every city had a pool of chronically unemployed or irregularly employed men, unskilled workers in trades where the level of demand for their services fluctuated by the day or the hour — the docks, the building industry, shipping. Very often the circumstances of their occasional opportunity of employment necessitated that they live close to the possibility of work, which led to overcrowding. Unemployment was recognised as one of the root causes of poverty and thus of poor physique. Despite some amelioration infant mortality remained high, as high as 200 per 1,000 in the Potteries where many women were engaged in arduous industrial work. The unsatisfactory economic, social and domestic environment in which most of the working class still lived in 1900 may have been necessary for mid-Victorian economic expansion, but that this need not continue to be so — need never have been so? — and that it was an affront to the conscience of a rich and Christian society was beginning to be recognised by 1900.

It is then scarcely surprising that contemporary social critics and commentators were disenchanted with the urban scene. London was particularly singled out — 'some voiceless prophet mutely pointing to the strange wounds and scars upon its face . . . the price paid for its greatness'.[8] Lawrence went so far as to introduce the concept of 'towniness' into his 'model' of housing problems[9] indicating a distaste not merely for the material aspects of urban life but for the very phenomenon. Even in Masterman, the radical and the social reformer, there are shades of Arnold or Ruskin: 'civilize the poor . . . expand their tiny rubbish yards into green gardens, introduce bow windows before and behind; remove from them the actual experience of privation, convert all England into a suburban city — will the completed product be pronounced to be "very good"?'[10] A consequence of such, if less sceptical, attitudes was the countrification of the city: 'England would one day be a huge garden city . . . we find whole village-like new communities created in this great era of domestic and rustic architecture.'[11] But not for the poor.

Ironically the idealisation and idolisation of the countryside, the preaching if rarely the practising of 'back to the land' as a solution for a mass of social and economic problems, coincided with agricultural crisis. The countryside which was worshipped did not exist and had never existed. The reality of 1900 was a slowly waning 20-year old agricultural depression — 1900 itself was a very unprosperous year — rural depopulation and emigration, and a rural labour force as ever the worst paid such group in Britain.[12] Reputedly, if not one suspects everywhere in reality, a deadweight of apathy, decay and inertia had settled like some pestilence over each and every village and hamlet. The illusion that all was well did not even begin to exist save for the privileged few in rural Britain at the end of the nineteenth century.

There were areas of national life which stood up to scrutiny rather better than the economy, the towns and the countryside. Britain had become almost wholly literate in the last quarter of the nineteenth century, a process in which very ancient regional differences disappeared, and an educational system had been set up which achieved this end and which was a contentious issue only on the limited sectarian front. A penny post, a national

Press — potent counterweights to regional isolation if not to regional identity — had been created; there was a superb railway system, worldwide dominance in shipping and, in many areas, at least an adequate system of suburban transport. 'From a collection of regions, separated rather than united by such means of transport as existed, England was becoming unified in a way never possible before.'[13] There were even some commentators who took an optimistic view of economic prospects: it was an American who wrote in 1911 'it is very doubtful whether its [Lancashire cotton] presence and influence in the world markets can be seriously affected, at least for many years to come'.[14]

If there had been a change of heart and mind from mid-century complacency it was evidently set in a context of even more complete geographical upheaval during the course of the century. Comparison with the past gave even Masterman grounds for optimism — 'who could be pessimistic who had traced the history of a hundred years, and compared the England of 1811 with the England of today?'[15] — and it provides the geographer of the 1970s with an appropriate framework with which to conclude a study of nineteenth-century Britain. What were the chief alterations in the geography of Britain between 1800 and 1900?

Britain had ceased to be predominantly rural and had become overwhelmingly urban and industrial. Of course in simple spatial terms Britain remained rural, and, as has been noted, urbanisation was less than wholeheartedly accepted. (A visual comparison of even the depressed countryside of the 1890s with either the manufacturing or residential quarter of a British town at the same date makes it easy to understand why.) By 1900 a mere nine per cent of the populace was in farming and thus the sacrifice of agricultural prosperity to urban well-being, whether or not it was necessary, proved politically palatable. The sacrifice itself depended upon a set of new geographical circumstances, the availability of food from overseas and the Pax Brittanica.

Urbanisation and industrialisation thus epitomise nineteenth-century Britain and the component parts of these developments have made up much of the preceding chapters of this book. Early in the century textiles, the old woollen trade and the new cotton trade, situated for the most part on the margins of the

Pennines, were dominant. Neither diminished in absolute importance during the century and cotton was spectacularly a growth industry, but by 1900 coal and steel occupied pride of place on the industrial scene. An industrial geographer of the period could not neglect Yorkshire and Lancashire but he might be expected first to give his attention to the Clyde, the Tyne and South Wales. Mackinder picked out Middlesborough, Barrow (and Belfast) as the growth centres of his time,[16] steel and shipbuilding towns close to indigenous ores and a little removed from the coalfields.

Coal was commercial king but locationally it was a spent force. One of the more surprising — and more forgotten — aspects of nineteenth-century Britain is how short was the period during which coal was a powerful force for industrial concentration, the brevity of the era between the triumph of the stationary steam engine and the establishment of a widespread railway network. In Mackinder's prescient summary, 'two generations ago men took the raw materials to be manufactured upon the coalfield; one generation ago they began to carry coal to the deposits of the raw material . . . it now appears likely that they will distil power from the coal at the pit mouth'.[17] Only cotton and wool were in that short era securely and rather exclusively tied to coalfield locations — as it happened to second-rank and early depleted coalfields. Iron and chemicals went through a phrase of coalfield fixation, aided in the former case by the black band ores, but new technologies, inside and outside the industries themselves, took them else-where in the second half of the century. Footloose industry is in fact a child of the Victorian railways as much as of twentieth-century dynamos and internal combustion engines. In some cases the absence of coal — and coalfield wage levels — appears to have been a boon to manufacturers seeking to implement new methods. By 1900 Britain's premier geographer could not only refer to coal exports as 'decentralisation . . . on an international scale'[18] but point to the re-emergence of old provincial towns and cities, Norwich and Northampton for example, in specialised industrial roles.

London had been recognised as a distinctive urban pheno-menon at and even before the start of the nineteenth century, a prosperous and peerless commercial giant. Its peculiar domin-ance and worldwide role increased rather than diminished during the century even though other conurbations came into existence. It is however to these conurbations and to the manufacturing towns rather than to London that the student of the Victorian city and town *per se* turns for his examples, to Bradford or Birmingham, and then perhaps to Middlesborough or Millom.[19] Although the greatest of these cities had become veritable conurbations by 1900 they remained compact by comparison with their subsequent extension; nineteenth-century suburbanisation was pre-eminently a London phenomenon the creation not of the industrial but of the commercial and business activities'.[20] Whatever its spatial scale the development of residential segregation within cities was very much a nineteenth-century phenomenon, the departure of the upper, middle and even skilled artisan classes towards the periphery. What had occurred on a very limited social and geographical scale early in the century — the Clapham Evangelicals were very rich and by the end of the century Clapham was a largely working class inner suburb — became by 1900 the common-place of the commercial community. Lady Bell could take it for granted even of a new iron and steel town.[21]

Suburbanisation is one facet, one consequence, of a new mobility. The nineteenth century was the century of the horse and pedestrian, but late in the century the train, the bus, the tram and the bicycle became the everyday means of movement of a large proportion, albeit not necessarily a majority, of the population. More people became more mobile, and often with surprising suddenness. The increase in numbers was however losing its momentum just as widespread personal mobility arrived. A different kind of mobility was manifest in the continuous redistribution of the population onto the coalfields, old and new, and into a discontinuous industrial axis extending from Thames to Mersey or even Clyde. Over much of rural Britain these population changes were small, in terms of density, and inconspicuous compared with either localised urban growth or even occasionally spectacular rural depopul-ation, but it is this localisation which is the most distinctive and significant feature of the population geography of nineteenth-century Britain.

Of how many Britains then is it legitimate to speak at the turn of the century? Social commentators leave their readers in no doubt as to the continuance of Disraeli's 'two nations' — rich and poor — and the phrase has remained in the political vocabulary. Mackinder chose to echo the *Géographie Universelle* in contrasting metropolitan and industrial Britain,[22] the coal-less and continental oriented south and east with the coal-rich cities and towns of the north and west. This is to emphasise the continuity of the very ancient lowland-highland dichotomy and a geographer of the 1970s might go on to interpret British entry to the European Common Market as a reassertion of metropolitan vitality after two centuries of more peripheral industrial vigour. To Mackinder however the nineteenth century was a period of developing balance between the two parts. Masterman, social critic and foe of that imperial outlook espoused by Mackinder, saw three Englands — and thus surprisingly little change since 1900 — 'there is rural England . . . there is urban England . . . never far from green fields . . . there is London: a population, a nation in itself'.[23] The distant perspective of the 1970s suggests four categories: London, the conurbations and smaller communities created by the century's staple industries for the most part in the north and west, the old provincial towns and cities beginning to experience revival by the last decades of the century, and finally the unprosperous — and forgotten — countryside. But late nineteenth-century Britain, however introspective, was not an essentially inward-looking society. Free trader and imperialist alike recognised that 40 million people living on a small island must needs carry on business with the world at large. This was the realm in which nineteenth-century Britain, the Victorian in particular, was pre-eminently successful; it was from this source that the wealth which enabled the transformation of landscape, economy and society — however unfortunate some aspects of that transformation appear to us — was drawn.

'It would be bold to hazard a prediction as regards England's position as a great power in the immediate future. Her interests are more complex, and through her numerous colonies she is brought into direct contact with a greater variety of nations than can be said of any other state in the world, ancient or modern. Not an event or commercial crisis can take place in any part of the world without England being affected by it. No other state organism is equally sensitive to outside impressions and the fate of Great Britain depends more or less upon the destinies of all those nations with which it entertains commercial relations'.[24]

Reclus' summary of 1886 requires modification on points of detail in 1975, but in general terms it remains as true for Britain entering the last quarter of the twentieth as for the last quarter of the nineteenth century.

NOTES

1 Bell, Lady Florence *At the works*, pp. 10-11. She considered her task as 'to put a piece of prosperity under the microscope' (p. 14), a useful corrective to the gloomy outlook usually ascribed to such writers. The best known of the genre is Charles Booth, *Life and Labour of the People in London*, London, 1891-1903.

2 'The geographical ideas, both true and false, of all manner of people . . . it necessarily has to do in large degree with subjective conceptions.' J.K. Wright. 'Terrae Incognitae: the place of the imagination in geography', *Annals of the Association of American Geographers*, vol. 38, 1947, pp. 1-15.

3 This is a curious, alternating mixture of modern systematic geography and guide-book topography reminiscent of the early nineteenth century.

4 Masterman, C.F.G., *The Heart of the Empire*, p. xx (of author's preface), quoting Mackail, J.W., *William Morris*, a lecture to the City of London, I.L.P., 1901.

5 Taylor, A.J., in Nowell-Smith, S. (ed.), *Edwardian England 1901-1914*, p. 107.

6 As defined by the Registrar General.

7 Discussed in the editorial introduction (Gilbert, B.B.,) to the 1973 reprint of *The Heart of the Empire* pp. xxiv-xxv. The matter became something of a national scandal.

8 Masterman, C.F.G. (ed.), *op.cit.*, p. 112 (in a chapter by Bray, R.A.).

9 Masterman, C.F.G. (ed.), *op.cit.*, p. 55. (in a chapter by Lawrence, F.W.).

10 Masterman, C.F.G., *The Condition of England*, p. 77.

11 Betjeman, J., in Nowell-Smith, S., op.cit., p. 365.

12 A realistic and reasonably objective survey is Haggard, H. Rider, *Rural England*, 1902.
13 Reader, W.J., *Life in Victorian England*, 1964, p. 162.
14 Quoted by Barker, T.C., in Cox, C.B., and Dyson, A.E. (eds), *The Twentieth Century Mind*, p. 61.
15 Masterman, C.F.G., *The Condition of England*, preface to 1911 edition.
16 Mackinder, H.J., *Britain and the British Seas*, 1902, pp. 328-9.
17 ibid., p. 339.
18 ibid p. 329.
19 Briggs, Asa, *Victorian Cities*, 1963, chooses to consider Manchester, Birmingham, Leeds, Middlesborough, Melbourne and London.
20 Masterman, C.F.G., *The Condition of England*, p. 69.
21 Bell, Lady Florence, *At the works*, p. 30.
22 Mackinder, op.cit., titles of chapters 14 and 15: Réclus, E., *The British Isles (Géographie Universelle)*, 1887, p. 486.
23 Masterman, C.F.G., *The Condition of England*, p. 99.
24 Reclus, op. cit., p. 486.

FURTHER READING

Cox, C.B., and Dyson, A.E. (eds), *The Twentieth Century Mind*, London, 1972 (especially Barker, T.C., 'History: economic and social', pp. 51-89).
Mackinder, H.J., *Britain and the British Seas*, London, 1902.
Masterman, C.F.G., *The Condition of England*, London, 1909.
Masterman, C.F.G. (ed.), *The Heart of the Empire*, London, 1901
Nowell-Smith, S. (ed.), *Edwardian England 1901-1914*, London, 1964. (especially Taylor, A.J., 'The economy', pp. 103-38).
Réclus, E. (trans. and ed. Ravenstein, E.G.), *The British Isles* (being volume 4 of *Géographie Universelle*), London, 1887.

Index